MY WORLD

JONNY WILKINSON

headline

First published in 2004
by HEADLINE BOOK PUBLISHING

10 9 8 7 6 5 4 3 2 1

Cataloguing in Publication Data is available from the British Library

ISBN 0 7472 4276 3

Typeset in Bliss, Bureau Gothic and letterpress fonts from Chank.com

Printed and bound in Great Britain by Butler & Tanner

Headline's policy is to use papers that are natural, renewable and
recyclable products and made from wood grown in sustainable
forests. The logging and manufacturing processes are expected to
conform to the environmental regulations of the country of origin.

Designed by Perfect Bound Ltd

HEADLINE BOOK PUBLISHING
A division of Hodder Headline
338 Euston Road
London NW1 3BH

www.headline.co.uk
www.hodderheadline.com

Contents

Acknowledgements

In putting together this book my thanks go to my mum and dad for their constant unconditional love and support, and to my brother for his humour and for always being there for me. Thanks also to Steve Black for his amazing dedication and ambition and to Tim Buttimore, Simon Cohen and Brendan Sargeant for their professional and selfless approach to organising me, as well as to my ghost, Neil Squires, for his effort and friendship. Finally, thank you to all my team-mates and coaches who work tirelessly to fulfil the dreams of Newcastle and England, and to all the England fans for their incredible support and impeccable behaviour.

Introduction

'I can't always succeed but I can always deserve to'

Jonny Wilkinson

I don't mind training alone, in fact I like it, but when you are your own boss as much as I am it is so easy to take a short cut, to knock off early. When the rain is pouring down on another cold Newcastle night and the wind is howling around Kingston Park, the temptation is always there to pack the bag of balls in the back seat of the car, head home from the training ground and put my feet up. After all, who would know?

I would. Cutting corners is not my way. I reason like this: if I train harder and better than anyone else, I will come out on top. Others might get lucky every now and again but the way I look at it life has to provide a reward for all the effort in the end.

This approach means I have to forego pleasures many twenty-five-year-olds take for granted but if I want to be true to myself and my team-mates I have no choice in my mind. To be the player I want to be for Newcastle or England I need to be sure the foundations for success are all in place. If that entails making sacrifices to spend more time on the training field so be it. Preparation is power.

By the time of the final, I had probably kicked something like 7,000 drop goals in four months

I cannot accept that the drop goal which won the 2003 Rugby World Cup final was just some random bolt out of the blue. It was the result of years of practice. Before the tournament England put themselves through the most demanding fitness programme the squad had ever undertaken. I did the same with my kicking. I have always worked my hardest, but ahead of the most important tournament of my career, I wanted to find a way to do more.

At the end of a light day's training – and I use the term relatively – I would work on my place kicking, grooving my routine for when it would be tested under the most severe pressure I have ever known. There was no time limit on the sessions – some lasted for three hours. After a heavy day's training, I would work on my drop kicks. I would kick at least twenty with my left foot and twenty with my right. Then I would practise my restarts. The process would be repeated again, and again, and again until I was happy.

All the kicking took its toll. My boots are specially made from casts of my feet so they fit like slippers but I had to keep having new casts made because my feet changed shape with the constant battering. When the squad went home for days off, I would go through the process each day on my own at Newcastle United's indoor training facility at Darsley Park. Bang, bang, bang. Ball after ball aimed at a three-inch-wide metal bar, doing my best to make sure that if the moment came in the World Cup I would be ready.

During the tournament itself, I made sure I hit forty drop goals every day, twenty off each foot, so by the time of the final, I had probably kicked something like 7,000 drop goals in four months. Obsessive? Maybe. Necessary? Definitely.

I play the odds – the harder I work, the more likely I am to succeed. All the practice doesn't guarantee success – against Australia I missed with my first three drop goal attempts – but the scales have to balance eventually. It's like an equation – what I get out has to match the amount of energy I put in. The fourth one, with my right boot, went over. You may have seen it.

That kick didn't change the way I approach rugby but it did change the way people approach me. I am slowly coming to terms with the fact that my life will never be quite the same again.

I play the odds –

the harder I work, the more likely I am to succeed

THE JO

URNEY

'Destiny is no matter of chance. It is a matter of choice.'

William Jennings Bryan

I **thought I understood** the intensity of international rugby until the 2003 World Cup. I believed I had reached a level that could not be surpassed in the quarter-final of the previous tournament against South Africa which England lost. All the hype, all the tension – the sheer scale of the event surely could not be eclipsed? I know better now. The knockout matches in Australia left that quarter-final for dead. They were more than rugby experiences, they were life experiences.

The defeat in 1999 by the Springboks proved England weren't ready to win a World Cup. That point was underlined in the years of squandered Grand Slams which followed. Yet all the time we were learning, filing away the knowledge gained from the disappointments and setbacks and using it to become a side that could win a World Cup.

The game against South Africa in Perth was again deemed our critical match in 2003 because it was the pool game which would logically send us along what was perceived to be the easier path into the knockout stages if we won. If results panned out as expected, we would avoid New Zealand in the quarter-final. The stakes, and the expectations engendered by our 53-3 win over a weakened

Springboks side at Twickenham the last time the sides had met, made for a horribly twitchy build-up. The two squads met at a World Cup launch in Perth and largely ignored each other. We all knew what was resting on the game.

Our preparations were disrupted by injuries, with Richard Hill and Matt Dawson ruled out and Kyran Bracken doubtful all week because of a back spasm. He came through in the end and so did we. It was an extremely tense, incredibly physical contest, the equal in intensity of that game four years previously, but this time we won 25-6.

The Springboks' fly-half Louis Koen, a fine goal-kicker, uncharacteristically missed three chances in the first half which allowed us to go into the break level. We were fortunate to be in that position – we had created little and made too many mistakes – but from there we took some semblance of control, riding out the South African storm and easing ahead as they ran out of steam. Will Greenwood touched down for our crucial try seventeen minutes from time after Lewis Moody had charged down Koen's clearance kick, I kicked my goals and we defended like our lives depended on it. Job done. It wasn't pretty but it was pretty effective.

Coming on top of our opening victory against Georgia, beating the Springboks put us in the position we wanted to be in and there was a brief but tangible feeling of relief within the squad. But it was like reaching a false summit. Far from conquering the mountain, we found that it just went up and up even more steeply from there.

The subconscious notion that we could relax a little after South Africa before the heavy-duty tests later in the tournament was smashed to smithereens by Samoa in Melbourne. There had been controversy before the World Cup over the absence of some of their top players like Trevor Leota, who had stayed to play for Wasps instead. The no-shows might have left them weak, some critics thought. They reckoned without the fact that the Samoans are the most natural rugby players on the planet.

We had a fair idea of what was coming from them and in training before the game the management asked the shadow squad to play as we believed the Samoans would – fast and furious. It was quite embarrassing. They gave us the runaround, with Mike Catt pulling the strings with his long passes

The Samoans
stretched us
every which
way with
their break-
neck rugby

and Trevor Woodman running like an outside back. We consoled ourselves with the thought that the Samoans wouldn't be as good and that the ball could never come back from the breakdown as fast as in that session. They were bound to drop some balls. Fat chance. They spilled so few they were 22-20 up with twenty minutes left.

There was an omen that all might not go well beforehand. The last thing I do before heading for the dressing room for our final team talk is to line up one easy confidence-boosting kick at goal from in front of the posts. I had to take three before the Samoa game because I was so unimpressed with the first two. Lo and behold I missed for the first time in the tournament early on in the game with a 50:50 long shot and then failed with a penalty from just to the left of the posts. I couldn't even blame the wind – the Telstra Dome's roof was closed. I knew from the moment of impact that the ball was heading for the upright; it was just a question of whether it would take a lucky ricochet. It didn't.

I could hear the murmur of the crowd afterwards – I couldn't pick up what they were saying but I could imagine. 'The pressure has got to him – he's bottling it.' It was just a simple technical error which was to blame but for all the crowd knew I was imploding. The neutrals in the Telstra Dome loved it. They were revelling in seeing us have our backsides bitten by the underdogs. The miss seemed to sum up an evening which was not going to plan for England to say the least.

We found ourselves chasing shadows. Samoa's stand-off, Earl Va'a, was magnificent, varying the play with kicks, breaks and long passes and the athleticism of some of their forwards was more like that of backs. The Samoans stretched us every which way with their break-neck rugby. I was hurtling across the pitch from one side to another to try to provide defensive cover outside the forwards and I felt heavy-legged. I had so little left that I couldn't fully impose myself in attack. I was having to grow a third eye to avoid Brian Lima, known affectionately as The Chiropractor for his bone-rearranging hits, who was trying to blow a hole in me. I didn't know what I had missed out on until I saw South Africa's Derick Houggard turn a full somersault on the receiving end of one of his beautifully timed one-way collisions the following week.

Coming back in those circumstances, when it felt like the world was against us, should not be underestimated

The force was with the Samoans and our World Cup was slipping away. Crucially, though, we clung on to our composure and hung in there. Gradually we hauled ourselves out of an almighty hole. It wasn't easy when the rope was fraying so badly but our resolve pulled us through. Iain Balshaw picked off a cross-kick of mine in full stride to go in for one try, Phil Vickery stepped his way over for a cracker and we were safe. The final whistle, when it came, was a blessed relief.

Coming back in those circumstances, when it felt like the world was against us, to win 35-22 should not be underestimated. Given how much trouble we were in, I would rate England's comeback as better than when we overhauled a twelve-point deficit to beat Australia at Twickenham the previous year. Nevertheless, we had been forced to dig deeper than we could have imagined against Samoa just to keep on course and that was a big concern. Far from the job being done by beating South Africa, the game against the Samoans underlined that it had hardly started.

A crunch meeting was called ahead of our next game against Uruguay, one that was to shape the rest of our World Cup. It was held at our base at Surfers Paradise on the Gold Coast. Clive Woodward, all the coaches and the key decision-makers – Martin Johnson, Lawrence Dallaglio, Will Greenwood, Phil Vickery, Neil Back, Matt Dawson and I – were there. We sat around tables on three sides of the meeting room while our coach, Andy Robinson, noted everything down on a flipchart at the front.

We were honest with each other. We had beaten South Africa and Samoa but had looked nothing like the England side we knew. We weren't thinking correctly. We use key words and phrases in the England set-up to dictate how we want to play. Nothing earth-shattering – words like 'ruthless', 'direct' or 'possession control' – but terms which, combined with coaching, are brought together to produce a style of play. People were not responding to the language and the result was that the game plan was staying behind in the dressing room. The responses needed sorting out.

We were attacking too narrowly and cutting down our range of options. A lot of it was down to over-keenness. This tournament was the culmination of four years' work and our anxiety to perform was proving to be self-defeating. Players were clattering into rucks all over the place and joining blind-side attacks out of a heightened desire to get involved, leaving us short of numbers to attack in the open spaces when the ball came back. This left us predictable and therefore vulnerable to aggressive defence and turnovers.

I was guilty of it myself to a degree. Clive felt I was over-committing myself clearing out rucks when I should have been leaving those duties to the likes of Backy. He stressed that as the play-maker I was of no use to the side trapped under a pile of bodies at the bottom of a ruck. I could see the logic in what he said but it is difficult when you are right beside a tackled colleague – your first instinct is to go in to protect him and the ball. If I could be of use in a physical sense I wanted to be in there. It didn't come naturally to let others do the work.

I was aware from my press conference appearances in Australia that people had been critical of how I was playing but since I went out of my way not to watch any of the television coverage or read any of the newspapers this hadn't had much impact. Sometimes, if a team-mate was reading a paper at breakfast, I would catch the odd headline by mistake but I would just go to sit somewhere else. In any case I was only really bothered about how my peers viewed my performances. Clive was publicly supportive but he was concerned about the strangulating pressure I was under, pressure that I was largely creating myself. I wanted to win the World Cup so much that I could think about little else.

Fatigue was a problem. I had never felt so tired playing rugby in my life. On top of training, I was kicking every day for up to three hours, as well as attending all the meetings. And when most were thinking about turning in for the night I would return to the team room to analyse our opponents on video over and over again. I made page after page of notes, detailing which foot every opponent preferred to step off, which arm they carried the ball under, everything you could think of. The rainforests took a real hammering. I was over-analysing everything in my head, but I believed it would make the difference if it could help me make a

Clive was publicly supportive but he was concerned about the strangulating pressure I was under

Locked inside my tunnel, the worries mounted up and from the most unexpected of sources

try-saving tackle. Rooming on my own, I was becoming a recluse. What spare time I had was spent watching trashy television. I was glad when October changed to November and with it the film selection in my hotel room. I'd watched all of them. Even the guitar sessions with the maestro Paul Grayson, which I had come to use as an escape, weren't quite working any more. I couldn't let go.

Locked inside my tunnel, the worries mounted up and from the most unexpected of sources. After our regulation victory over the amateurs from Uruguay in Brisbane in the next pool match, we sat on the bus on the way back to the team hotel and listened on the radio to Wales's game against New Zealand. What was going on in Sydney was unbelievable. The Welsh, who had struggled through their pool matches, had suddenly come alive and were threatening the shock of the tournament.

We had banked on a quarter-final against Wales since we had beaten South Africa but with fifteen minutes left they were ahead and we were staring at a knockout game against New Zealand in a week's time. We had worked so hard through adversity to get past the Springboks and Samoa and now it seemed our best-laid plans were going up in smoke, with us unable to do anything about it.

I couldn't bear to listen to the commentary – I felt so helpless – but I was outvoted forty to one so I had to sit there and hear our fate being decided hundreds of miles away. At least when things were going wrong against Samoa I could take an active part in trying to sort things out. Now my hands were tied and that was a horrendous feeling. In the end New Zealand prevailed but Wales had served notice of what they were capable of and they were to give us another agonising examination in the quarter-final.

The way the Samoans had played against us had served as a warning of what was to come – we thought Wales were bound to employ the same tactics, and it came as no surprise to us when they did. Not that we did much about it. Riddled with anxiety, our response was equally inadequate in the first half and at the interval we were 10-3 down. It could have been more – Wales had given us the runaround.

We were blowing hard in the dressing room but Clive and Andy sat us down and calmly reiterated their confidence in us, spelling out the way we were going to play and how we were going to re-take control of the game. 'If we play the game in their half and take care of the ball when we get hold of it we will break them down and win,' was the message and to a man we all knew it was true. There were no dire warnings of what would happen if we didn't, no panic, just

a professional measured response to the crisis that faced us. Those words were so important. We were on the ropes at the time but after the break the confidence seemed to seep back into us, and with Mike Catt coming on to help dictate the play, we hit back again and won 28-17. Jason Robinson set up a great try for Will just after half-time with a superb piece of counter-attacking and Wales's propensity to give away penalties under pressure allowed us to pull clear. The long-range drop goal with which I finished the game was undoubtedly my favourite one of the tournament. It was my sleeping pill for that night.

The long-range drop goal with which I finished the game was undoubtedly my favourite one of the tournament

I'm convinced we would have lost that match in previous seasons. The impetus, like in the Samoa game, had been with Wales and in those Grand Slam defeats we had been unable to find a way of reversing it. However, by the World Cup we had become an extremely experienced side – the starting fifteen against Wales had a world-record 689 caps – and we used every last bit of that combined knowledge to adapt and adjust under severe pressure.

Allied to our response against Samoa, the way in which we reacted in the quarter-final underlined to me that we had within us what it would take to win the World Cup. It was still going to take a mighty effort, of course, because we weren't playing with the freedom we wanted. The matches to come and everything which surrounded them would be colossal but I just felt we had been through too much at the tournament to fail. The game in Brisbane against the Welsh added another coating of steel around us and I don't think we looked back after that. When the critics judged another narrow squeak a sign of fallibility they misread the tea leaves. The more important fact was this: we had come through the examination – our third towering challenge of the tournament – intact and were still afloat, heading for the semi-finals.

The Australian media made a big issue of the fact that Wales had outscored us in tries and labelled us boring. I was asked about whether penalties should be worth fewer points. It was ridiculous. If teams stop you playing by giving away penalties, you kick them. I was just baffled to hear people talking about whether or not the laws were correct in the middle of a World Cup tournament.

I had as much chance of a dip in the sea as Clive did of becoming Australian Prime Minister

When we reached Sydney, one of the papers even printed 'stop boring rugby' T-shirts and conned me into posing for a photo to back their campaign. The T-shirts featured a picture of me goal-kicking with a diagonal red line plastered across it. Their reporter held out his hand for me to shake on the way out of a press conference and, not wanting to appear off-hand, I did. The telltale click of the camera and a quick glance at the T-shirt told me I'd been had, good and proper. I could just imagine him exchanging high-fives with his photographer as I walked off, nervously anticipating what tomorrow morning's edition would bring.

What this all showed, as well as a good imagination, was that the Australians were worried. Clive, who had lived out in Australia for five years, warned us what was coming from the local media and lapped it all up. When I sat alongside him at the press conference after the Wales victory, he confronted the sniping head on. He just stated in plain and simple English that we were going to Sydney to play France in the semi-final and that we would beat them. End of story. It is terrific when someone has that level of belief in you and when you know that he means it. There were no mind games here.

Arriving in Sydney meant diving into the epicentre of the World Cup. It had been a superbly supported tournament, embraced enthusiastically everywhere we had gone across Australia but this was where the mercury shot out of the thermometer. When a giant rugby ball lights up the Sydney Harbour Bridge, you know you are in the middle of something special.

The huge number of English supporters had swollen further, meaning our hotel, looking out through the pines onto the beautiful Manly Beach, was besieged. I had as much chance of a dip in the sea as Clive did of becoming Australian Prime Minister.

Richard Hill was back to fitness for the semi-final. He and I take great pleasure in sharing an inconsequential afternoon together a couple of days before a match, just strolling to a café or a clothes shop and chatting about anything other than rugby. Unfortunately that was not possible in the circumstances – we would have been buried in the crush. Not even my unofficial minder, our scrum coach Phil Keith-Roach, who had taken to accompanying me in public because I was so

The support
was both
inspiring and
terrifying.
Seeing all
those England
flags and
jerseys was
a great lift

useless at saying no to autograph hunters, would have been any use.

The support was both inspiring and terrifying. Seeing all those England flags and jerseys was a great lift a long way from home, after six weeks away, but it also gave us an inkling of just how many people we would be letting down if we lost. For a side that had exhibited signs of tension throughout the tournament that was a heavy burden to carry.

What helped us a great deal, though, in a one-off match where we lived and died by the result, was the way France were being talked up. They had become the darlings of the media during the tournament, throwing open the doors of their hotel overlooking Bondi Beach at all hours to all comers. That same media, we were told, were making them favourites on the back of our struggles and the great rugby France had played in sweeping aside Ireland 43-21 in the quarter-final. Some bookmakers had followed suit.

Our aim had always been to travel to Australia as favourites because that meant we were, in theory, the best team there but the label had put us in straitjackets. There is no doubt we were feeling inhibited. It is curious that a side sometimes plays differently when they are expected to win. They tend to try not to lose with risk-free rugby, placing more emphasis on making the right decisions than just playing naturally. That had been the case with England.

But with the weight of expectation lessening a little on the back of France's billing, there was a noticeable change in the atmosphere in our camp as the week wore on. It was reflected in training – the team runs were shorter and sharper, the minds less woolly. The nerves were still a constant companion hammering away at me – this was a World Cup semi-final after all, a forbidding place I had never been before – but I had such faith in the men around me that I felt like I could face my fear.

We knew what we had to do and we went and did it

I had also discovered a temporary escape from all the suffocating anxiety. Steve Black, my fitness conditioner at Newcastle, sent me out two detective novels by Michael Connelly and I lost myself in the cases of private investigator Harry Bosch. I am not a big reader usually but in the claustrophobic situation I was in, unable to escape from the hotel except for training, I cherished my time inside the pages of *Angel's Flight* and *The Black Ice* with an irrational passion. They were my comfort blankets. I used to lie in my room and allow myself to be taken away by the words, away from all the madness building up outside the hotel and the responsibility, away from rugby itself. Occasionally I would glance at the clock. You would not believe the joy I experienced from seeing I had lost half an hour in the book and still had half an hour spare to indulge myself before a team meeting or dinner. A big part of international rugby is about being comfortable. It is such an unnatural and demanding environment that anything you can grab hold of to make you feel calm and relaxed is helpful.

Some critics have said France were beaten by the weather in the semi-final, but I was just as disappointed as they no doubt were when I pulled back the curtains and saw the rain coming down. We had trained to explode onto the pitch that week and to know we would now have to play a limited game was deflating. No matter. We knew what we had to do and we went and did it.

The conditions were much the same as at Murrayfield in 2000 when we had blown a Grand Slam. People said we tried to play too much rugby that day – an argument which grossly over-simplified the problem and that I never agreed with – but we had developed to the stage where we knew what was required in the wet.

The forwards were magnificent – their strength and investment were phenomenal – and if you needed a visible illustration of what was to come from them, the sight of tears streaming down Lawrence's face during the anthems said it all. We had worked on our set piece ahead of the game, knowing the threat the French scrum and line-out posed to the basics of all our ball winning, and we countered it superbly. Every piece of possession the French backs received seemed to be on the back foot which made life very hard for Frederic Michalak, their young fly-half who had enjoyed such a fabulous tournament. In contrast, when we got hold of the ball we were going forward, so it was that much easier for either me or Catty to drill them back. Even though we conceded an early lead again, this time to a Serge Betsen try, we were able to put ourselves in the positions to keep the scoreboard moving and we eventually got out of sight.

The conditions were bad for kicking – there was a strong, swirling wind as well as rain – but I had encountered worse in Newcastle. I trusted my technique and it held up. Likewise with the three drop goals – any method of keeping the scoreboard moving and of rewarding our forwards for their relentless toil was valuable. Putting France in the position where they needed to score tries to win in those conditions was our aim and we managed it. In the end they ran out of ideas. Having established a 24-7 lead, I was actually able to enjoy the last five minutes of the semi-final, to bask in pressure-free rugby played out in front of a fantastic wall of English support. Aside from the Georgia match, they were about the only five minutes of the tournament in which I felt able to relax. We knew at that point we would be back in the Telstra Stadium the following weekend.

The conditions were bad for kicking – there was a strong, swirling wind as well as rain – but I had encountered worse in Newcastle

It took all of about two seconds after the semi for me to start thinking about the final itself, the biggest game of my life

One of the great motivating factors for me in winning that semi-final was reaching the World Cup final but there was another bonus to be had from beating France – not playing in the third-place play-off. We had watched Australia beat New Zealand in the previous day's semi-final and as the All Blacks had traipsed off disconsolately at the end it had occurred to me what an appalling sense of anti-climax taking part in the play-off would have brought. I would have preferred to have gone straight home if we'd lost.

The Wallabies had headed off on a lap of honour after beating the All Blacks, but even though the stadium was bathed in white for our semi-final and our magnificent fans probably deserved a wave or two after being drenched by the rain, the thought never entered our heads. We had come to Australia to win a final, not a semi-final. The management called a 1 a.m. meeting after the game to reinforce that point but they need not have bothered. It took all of about two seconds after the semi for me to start thinking about the final itself, the biggest game of my life.

FINAL

'There's 35 seconds to go, this is the one. It's coming back to Jonny Wilkinson. He drops for World Cup glory...'

Ian Robertson

I am always nervous before a rugby match. I always have been. When I played mini-rugby as a ten-year-old I would go to bed the night before a game happy enough because I had the barrier of sleep between me and what I had to do the next day. I always slept well. But once I woke up, the anxiety would sweep over me. I would suffer panic attacks, the tears would flow and I would be consumed by a strong urge not to go through with it. To try to alleviate the symptoms, I used to set my alarm ridiculously early – 5 a.m. – so that I could turn over and go back to sleep, putting off the reality for another precious couple of hours. Waking up again at 7 a.m., the anguish would have subsided to a degree. By 8 a.m., after turning over for another hour, it was possible for me to contemplate going to the match. The tension would rise to the surface again on the way there. Dad would often have to stop the car for me to be sick. The condition wasn't physical fear – my favourite part of rugby, then as now, was tackling. Instead, it was the thought of losing and letting myself down at something which meant so much to me. The stress levels which that brought on were almost paralysing.

I have sat in stadia the world over before games, thinking to myself, 'Do I really want to do this? wouldn't life be so much easier if I didn't show up?'

Fourteen years on, I woke, for the second time, at 8 o'clock on the morning of 22 November, 2003, in the England team hotel feeling the familiar dread. My thoughts were a mixture of excitement, tension and a raging desire to run away from it all. I have sat in stadia the world over before games, thinking to myself, 'Do I really want to do this? Wouldn't life be so much easier if I didn't show up?' World Cup final or not, I didn't feel any differently. Overcoming the instinct to pull the duvet over my head and hide was hard. It had been a crazy week. The theme from the management had been to treat the match as just another game of rugby but all the other indicators were suggesting it was anything but. Everything surrounding the match was unreal.

The support had gone crazy. There were swathes of England fans outside our hotel at all hours. *The Times*, for whom I was writing a newspaper column, wanted me to pose for a picture by the sea a few days ahead of the game. The photographer took me to a beach he assured me would be quiet. I had my reservations, given that 50,000 Englishmen were in town, but, hidden by shades and cap, I dutifully went along. It was packed. A quick snap and you couldn't get me out of there fast enough.

The hotel fax
machine was in
danger of
burn-out with
all the good
luck messages
from home

The hotel fax machine was in danger of burn-out with all the good luck messages from home. Jack Charlton, a World Cup winner thirty-seven years before, sent his best wishes, as well as the Welsh and Irish teams. Most numbing of all was the weight of words from ordinary people.

The media interest had gone through the roof too. Hundreds of journalists, photographers, radio and TV people turned up for press conferences, not all of them maintaining objective neutrality. One Australian television crew decked out their camera with a big poster of the Wallabies for Clive to stare at as he answered their questions. One of the country's tabloid papers urged patriotic Australians to keep us awake the night before the final by making a racket outside the hotel. The same rag printed a cut-out-and-keep voodoo doll of me for people to stick pins into. Classy touch.

The media scrum had become so unwieldy when we left the hotel for training that we had taken to coming back via an underground car park in an attempt to sidestep all the camera crews. They soon got wind of it. On one occasion we ended up sprinting off the bus to the lift at the back entrance but because it took an age to descend they got plenty of footage of us hanging around awkwardly waiting for it. Best-laid plans and all that.

We trained lightly, not cutting corners but reflecting how much our quarter-final and semi-final had taken out of us. We had a day less to prepare than the Australians and we tried to conserve our energy. The forwards didn't do any scrummaging and we walked through a lot of our moves. The hard work had been done in pre-season and before the other matches. We had to trust that it was safely in the bank. We needed to be fresh for the challenge that lay ahead. After kicking, I rested as much as I could in my room, reading Harry Bosch. He had provided such comfort that when I finished the last page two days before the final, I seriously considered re-reading it. In the end I begged a book off Dave Reddin, our fitness coach. It didn't quite hold the same hypnotic power though.

On the night before the game we watched an England 'greatest hits' video. Clive spoke to us with passion about what was to come and as I left the room the nerves were jangling. In my pocket were two pieces of paper.

PLAY MY GAME
NOTHING CHANGES
BE THE BEST
GET WHAT YOU DESERVE

One was from Matt Dawson – a list of five key words for me to shout at him during the match to keep him on top of his game – and the other was the game plan. It was scribbled on a small piece of hotel notepaper. Part of it related to me, part to the team. This is what it said:

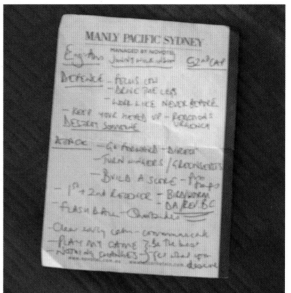

Eng-Aus, Jonny Wilkinson, 52nd cap

Defence
Alert, stay bouncing, head up
Make 100 per cent tackles – focus low, drive the legs
Incredible work rate – non-stop, get off the floor
Destroy someone – embarrass them

Attack
Direct – go forward
Kick on front foot when appropriate – turn wingers Sailor and Tuqiri
Use short sides
Build a score
Drop goal routine

There were words of advice and encouragement too:

Play my game
Nothing changes
Be the best
Get what you deserve

Around these bullet points were the names of the team plays and the calls I planned to make early in the game.

The bare bones of the game plan were to play the game in Australian territory and then keep the ball when we got there

The bare bones of the game plan were to play the game in Australian territory and then keep the ball when we got there. The Australians had an outstanding defence but we felt we had the edge in the front five and that we could wear them down by building phases and moving them around. Our general kicking game revolved around turning the Wallabies' wings to receive our kicks, thus making it more difficult for them to run the ball back at our defence. It was aimed at giving our kick chase time to organise itself. Neither Wendell Sailor nor Lote Tuqiri, who had both come from rugby league, were motivated to kick the ball and we backed our defensive system to cope with their counter-attack. Australia's full-back Mat Rogers had also come from league but while he was a good kicker off his left foot we thought we could reap rewards by forcing him to kick off his weaker right foot.

With these instructions safely tucked away, I went to bed knowing exactly how I would feel when I woke.

So it begins. On the morning of the final, I reluctantly leave the safety of my room and wander down to breakfast. I make small talk with my team-mates over cereal, toast and egg-white omelettes. I used to be silent on the morning of a match, wrapped up in what lay ahead, but I have improved to the extent that I can manage to converse with the outside world a little now. After breakfast, I go to the training ground in Manly with Dave Alred, the kicking coach, for an hour's 'nudging'. In amongst the punting and the place-kicks I practise twenty drop-kicks off each foot. The session goes well, although I still can't properly feel my feet on the floor because of the tension in my legs.

Back at the hotel, we have a team meeting to run over the weather forecast and check everyone is fit and healthy. Clive has taken no chances. On the day of the 1995 World Cup final, several All Blacks were affected by food poisoning so he had brought over our own chef, Dave Campbell, to keep an eye on things behind the scenes. We are all OK.

Johnno takes the forwards off for a word and I have a chat with the backs to run through our tactics. I stress the importance of communication. I tell them it is going to be noisy in the Telstra Stadium so we have to talk loudly and constantly to each other even though it will still be virtually impossible to hear a thing. Mentioning this is to state the obvious with 80,000 people there but the point behind it is to emphasise to the players that we will have to react almost by instinct to help each other out under the pressure of the occasion that awaits us. When we arrive at the stadium we cannot afford to be surprised by the atmosphere.

Before the quarter-final against Wales, the match twenty-two had gone for a stroll to loosen the muscles but, hemmed in by the wall of supporters, it is impossible this time. So after a light lunch, I return to my room and pack my bag. In go my shoulder pads, two kicking tees and three pairs of boots. Two are studded and one bladed. Then I try to relax on my bed. The 8 p.m. kick-off, Sydney time, leaves a lot of hours to fill but I like to watch the minutes tick by. It is preferable to the relative rush of an afternoon game.

I surface for my usual pre-match ritual of a shave and shower before settling down to listen to a mental rehearsal CD. The script is prepared by myself and Dave Alred but read by him – I don't want to doze off and miss the bus listening to myself droning on. This visualisation technique is a sort of clarified daydream with snippets of the atmosphere from past matches included to enhance the sense of reality. It lasts about twenty minutes and by the end of it I feel I know what is coming. The game will throw up many different scenarios but I am as prepared in my own head for them as I can be. If you have realistically imagined situations, you feel better prepared and less fearful of the unexpected.

I used to be silent on the morning of a match, wrapped up in what lay ahead, but I have improved to the extent that I can manage to converse with the outside world a little now

'Fill yourself with the warrior spirit – and send that warrior into action.'

Finally, before leaving the privacy of my own space, I dig out two faxes from Steve Black. The first one, which came during the knockout stages, encourages me, World Cup final or not, to go with my instincts. If it feels right, it is right, is his message.

'Go with your instinctive gut feeling and reasoned response – it hasn't let you down before. Have total belief in yourself and your internal guidance.'

It is almost like Blackie has been reading my mind. This is not a conversation we had ever had together but the words hit the nail on the head for me. Trusting your instincts is an integral part of feeling confident. I needed to know that the way I had been preparing was correct for me – from reading a book in the afternoon to kicking on the training field. I was worried about letting others down and I was concerned that if I blew this opportunity I would find it hard to live with the regret.

The other fax from Blackie arrived at the start of the tournament. It is one I have read on the day of each game at the World Cup. I read it through again. It is a speech delivered by General George S. Patton, the commander of the US Third Army in Europe, during World War II. I almost know it by heart now.

'Today you must do more than is required of you. Never think that you have done enough or that your job is finished. There's always something that can be done, something that can help to ensure victory. You can't let others be responsible for getting you started. You must be a self-starter. You must possess that spark of individual initiative that sets the leader apart from the led. Self-motivation is the key to being one step ahead of everyone else and standing head and shoulders above the crowd. Once you get going don't stop. Always be on the lookout for the chance to do something better. Never stop trying. Fill yourself with the warrior spirit – and send that warrior into action.'

* READ ON THE EVE + DAY of EACH GAME * SPD BLACK

FAO * JONNY WILKINSON *
PENNYHILL HOTEL

Dear Jonny,

this speech has gone down in history
as one of the most effective and
inspirational ever delivered to a team
of men. General Patton delivered this to his troops during
his phenomenally successful period as commanding general
of the Seventh Army. I have personally benefitted from
the passion of this oratory at numerous times throughout
My life. I hope it has the same effect for you.

                love + respect
                Blackie's lot

Today you must do more than is required of you. Never think
that you have done enough or that your job is finished. There's
always something that can be done — something that can help
to ensure victory. You can't let others be responsible for getting
you started.   You must be a self-starter. You must possess
that spark of individual initiative that sets the leader apart
from the led. Self-Motivation is the key to being one step
ahead of everyone else and standing head and shoulders above
the crowd. Once you get going don't stop. Always be on the
lookout for the chance to do something better. Never stop
trying. Fill yourself with the Warrior Spirit — and send that
Warrior into action.

                God Bless; Onwards + Upwards Blackie

I want to show myself that I am not going to be distracted by anything, good or bad, ahead of this game

I head down for our pre-match meal – chicken breast, mince and a couple of sandwiches for the carbohydrate levels. I burn energy very quickly, so, for all the nerves, I've never had a problem eating before a match. Even this match.

Andy runs through a few points with the squad before a final word from Clive and then we are off into the frenzy. There must be close to 1,000 people waiting for us, cheering us, applauding us. We are given a tumultuous reception – everywhere I look there are English flags – but I don't allow myself to acknowledge anyone. I want to show myself that I am not going to be distracted by anything, good or bad, ahead of this game. I think the fans would rather be given a World Cup than a smile.

Safely on the bus, I sit in my usual place, halfway back, and idle away the forty-minute journey to Homebush, picking the labels off my energy drinks. It is a subdued trip, through largely deserted suburban streets, before the storm to come. A special CD accompanies us en route. It has been compiled by Mike Tindall and is intended to finish with an inspirational tune as we arrive at the ground. Before the semi-final somebody fiddled with it and we pulled in to the stadium to the strains of 'Rock The Casbah' by The Clash. Close, but no cigar. This time the choreography is perfect and as the Telstra Stadium climbs spectacularly into view the England bus arrives to the strains of 'Lose Yourself' by Eminem.

It is a subdued trip, through largely deserted suburban streets, before the storm to come

I try to sit down but it's impossible. My legs won't keep still. I pace the changing room, talking to the backs, checking out how they are feeling and spelling out again what I need from them

I change quickly and, as always, have a brief flick through the match programme then head out onto the pitch to kick. When I return the tension is eating into every pore. I try to sit down but it's impossible. My legs won't keep still. I pace the changing room, talking to the backs, checking out how they are feeling and spelling out again what I need from them. I re-read my sheet of paper, over and over again.

The coaches do their bit and then we're out onto the field for the team warm-up. The atmosphere is building all around the stadium but it barely registers. I'm into it now. I am reassured by the knowledge I will have trained as hard, and in my mind harder, than anyone else on that pitch. I also know that when the whistle blows, a switch will flick inside me. Suddenly I will become incredibly competitive and ultra-aggressive. I will be inwardly driven to do anything to win this match. I put over my final kick and then return to the changing room. I check my piece of paper one last time, then spray glue on my hands to combat the evening dew.

It's just the players now. Johnno pulls us into a huddle. He talks passionately, telling us to look around at each other and remember the experiences we have been through together. This is our time. In the last year we have beaten everyone and overcome every challenge. It is this thought that we hold onto at this moment. Man for man we believe we are better than Australia, we have worked harder than they have for this moment and we are stronger — physically and mentally. It is the game of our lives and there must be no regrets afterwards. No ounce of effort must be left behind. Lawrence Dallaglio and Phil Vickery chip in. Beneath the expletives key points are being reinforced — it isn't just 'let's kick the hell out of them'. Nobody is punching or head-butting anyone. The fury is controlled. The aggression lurks just below the surface. It is there, though — I can feel it — and the adrenaline from that provides the last piece of comfort I need to go out there and attack the game. The thought of facing Australia in that furnace is frightening but exhilarating too.

Then it is time to go, time to leave the sanctuary of the changing room and time to face our destiny. We are held in a line, feet from the Wallabies, waiting for the signal to take the field together. In this situation, before every match I have ever played with him, Johnno has turned around and offered one final call to arms. He has the capacity to shock us and intimidate opponents with his venom and aggression and I wonder what he is going to say. The Australian players will hear it as well as us and with all the tension it would not take much to light the blue touch paper. Johnno turns around, fixes us with that beetle-browed stare and begins to open his mouth. But for the first time he does not say anything. That silence counts for a thousand words. He can see in our eyes that we are ready. I still wonder what that must have felt like for Australia.

We run out into a tumbling wall of noise thrown out by the vast banks of gold and white. It takes your breath away. The anthems follow — a very personal moment in a highly impersonal setting, with all those people looking on and a camera up my nose. Although I'm singing the words to 'God Save The Queen' loudly in my head they come out of my mouth as a quiet mumble. I am thinking about the important people in my life, about those who have helped to put me in that line. I am thinking about how fortunate I am to be playing for my country in a World Cup final. Most importantly, I'm thinking about the first play of the game. The music finishes, the crowd roars and after one

He has the capacity to shock us and intimidate opponents with his venom and aggression and I wonder what he is going to say

final huddle with Johnno we are away. Steve Larkham puts the ball into the sky against a backdrop of exploding flashlights and instantly all the nerves and all the anxiety melt away, just as they did when the whistle blew when I was a ten-year-old. I am just a rugby player playing in a rugby match again, I don't feel sick any more.

The game plan I have taken such care to memorise is more a starting point than a strict doctrine – you have to play what is in front of you on the pitch – and that point is underlined when the Wallabies take the lead. A brilliant cross-kick by Larkham puts Lote Tuqiri in an aerial battle with Jason Robinson and with a six-inch height advantage there is only one winner. Five-nil Australia.

We gather under the crossbar. There are no recriminations. It was a great play by the Wallabies and there is not much we could have done to prevent the try. We can hear the noise of the crowd but it doesn't affect us. I try to imagine what the stadium will sound like when we score. Within minutes we have done, with a penalty. Then another. Then another. We are into our stride.

Just before half-time comes a big moment. Mat Rogers kicks long, Jason runs the ball back and from the ruck in midfield suddenly everything opens up. Lawrence bursts off it and I hare after him, screaming for the pass back on the angle because, for the first time in the game, we have the Australians stretched and I can see a big hole opening up. He delays too long and goes into contact but with his strength he manages to get his arms out of the tackle and the ball away to me with one hand. I am one-on-one with Rogers, the last line of the Australian defence, but I can sense English support runners arriving on either side of me. In the tumult of the crowd, I can't hear Ben Cohen calling on my right or Jason on my left. It wouldn't matter if they had loudspeakers – in these situations peripheral vision has to take over. I have only a split second to make the decision. Twenty metres out, Ben has the ideal line to go between the posts but I reason that with the Australians' fantastic scramble defence a covering wing or George Gregan must be tracking him so I go for Jason. After delaying for a fraction to try to hold Rogers, the pass is delivered, he takes it and, with his

I try to imagine what the stadium will sound like when we score. Within minutes we have done, with a penalty.

Then another.

Then another.

We are into our stride

pace over a short distance and low, scuttling running style, there is simply no-one better to finish in that situation. Rogers can't get there and Jason slides over for the try. The place goes mad and so does Jason, punching the ball heavenwards.

The move in itself hadn't been planned — they rarely are — but neither had the try simply materialised out of nothing. It came late in a half when we had tired the Wallabies by draining them in the set piece and dragging them around the field. The success came from the whole team's understanding and reaction. It was a good effort for either side to have engineered a try. The defences were so strong, the desire so great, that even in an elongated game there were only six line breaks in 100 minutes of rugby.

Half-time comes – keep it going boys, don't stop playing, let's win the second half

Half-time comes — keep it going boys, don't stop playing, let's win the second half. Except Australia have other ideas. They chip away at us, punishing us for giving away silly penalties while keeping their own discipline superbly. I don't have one shot at goal in the second half. Elton Flatley pulls the score back to 14-11 but the clock is running down and we are keeping them out of range. We are within touching distance of the Webb Ellis Trophy. Then, disaster. Referee André Watson blows his whistle at a scrum. Penalty to Australia. Don't ask me to explain why — I don't know what goes on in a scrum. What is frustrating is that there is nothing us backs can do about it. In fact, despite being in the scrum, I think the forwards feel the same. The Wallabies have an escape route and up steps Flatley. One kick to keep his side in the World Cup.

I would have done anything to have to won that World Cup final in eighty minutes, to have spared myself the agonies of extra time but as Flatley lines up the ball I find myself thinking as a fellow kicker rather than an opponent. This is the kick we all train for, the one we visualise over and over, alone on the practice field. And under all the pressure in the world, he nails it. 'Fair play to you, my friend,' I mutter under my breath. If anything deserves to take a game into extra time, that kick does.

We are awarded a penalty almost immediately, right at the limit of my range. Johnno asks me if I think I can get it. I tell him I'll have a go.

I make it

So extra time it is – uncharted territory for everyone. Part of me wants to go over to the Wallabies and offer to share the cup but we've come too far for that. There must be a winner. And a loser. The rules are twenty minutes of extra time, followed by ten minutes of sudden-death rugby and then, God forbid, a drop goal shoot-out. I can't face that. Lining up a drop goal with defenders running at you is all very well in a match but in the sterile environment of a shoot-out, with the cup on the line, it would be totally unnerving. And how could I face myself if I missed?

As we mill around the pitch, thinking these thoughts and regrouping ourselves for one last push, it all feels strangely surreal. Standing there, out in the middle, waiting to go again, it's a bit like we're at some inconsequential sevens tournament rather than the World Cup final, if it wasn't for Revenge of The Nerves, Part Two. I half expect Clive to bring the oranges on. As it is he makes a beeline for me. He starts going on about us needing points to win this game – penalties and drop goals. 'No kidding Clive,' is my instinctive reaction but I bite my tongue. 'Kicking,' I'm thinking. 'I need to practise my kicking.' And I go off with a ball towards the posts. Clive is left standing there, talking to thin air. Not very polite, I know, but I'm aware of the score. If it will be a penalty or a drop goal that wins the World Cup, then I want the chance to check how I'm looking.

Johnno gathers us in again and exhorts us not to dwell on the last eighty minutes but to put everything into the next twenty. I've never been here before but the trick in situations like this must be to get two scores up and, unbowed by the disappointment of being pushed into extra time, we are awarded a penalty almost immediately, right at the limit of my range. Johnno asks me if I think I can get it. I tell him I'll have a go. I make it. Paul Grayson tells me afterwards that he could tell from the sound of the strike that it was over and he let the bench know way before the ball reached the posts. It is my best goal-kick of the tournament and gives us a three-point lead.

However, we cannot pull clear and spend our time trying to keep Australia out of penalty range. We know the referee has an itchy finger. We reach the break intact but, with the tension almost unbearable in the second period, Australia are awarded another penalty. Flatley does it again – 17-17. There is pandemonium in the stadium.

Near exhaustion and despair, I look up at the clock. We have three minutes – one shot, one opportunity.

Field position is everything so we make a quick decision to kick-off long, knowing Rogers will clear his lines and that we will have the line-out throw inside their half. I call 'Zig-zag' to Matt Dawson and he relays the code word to Ben Kay who will then call an appropriate line-out to enable us to activate the move. 'Zig-zag' is a move we have rehearsed many times, setting up the ideal position for a drop goal. It has been in the back of my mind all through the final; now it is right at the front.

We need a secure set piece — by no means guaranteed in a final where neither side have been able to dominate their own ball. Steve Thompson hits the button, picking out Lewis Moody at the tail, the hardest part of the line-out to find but obligatory for this attack. It allows us to launch Catty onto the ball and immediately over the gain-line. Australia know what we are planning and concentrate on getting up fast to charge down the drop goal but in doing so leave a hole for Matt Dawson to burst through the ruck. He is hauled down having made a crucial twenty metres — an awesome run for the team but don't mistake the fact that he was trying to score himself! He has put us in range and, back in the pocket, I scream for the ball thirty metres out, readying myself for the kick. I'm to the left of the posts so I line it up with my right foot to open up the angle and to avoid the charge-down. But Daws is buried and Backy is waiting to deliver the pass at scrum-half. Johnno sees this and, critically, takes the ball up one more time, making the Australian forwards defend again and allowing Daws to return to his station. The Wallabies go offside in their keenness to come through but the referee only warns them. Then I see Daws picking up the ball. I lift my hands to receive it and he fires back the perfect pass. This is it.

I know it doesn't have to go far; just straight. When I connect it feels good

The knack with a drop goal is to connect with the ball as it makes contact with the ground, turning it into a place-kick in effect. But when I drop the ball it lands slightly off-centre, bouncing fractionally towards me as I strike it. This reduces the power I can put through the ball but it actually makes accuracy easier. I know it doesn't have to go far; just straight. When I connect it feels good. Phil Waugh tries to block the kick but he can't get there – it's up and away into the sky. I look up, I see the posts and I know it is going between them. It does. After all the pain, all the sacrifice and all the hardship it might just be that England are going to win the World Cup.

Then I am seized by a moment of panic. Can the referee deny us again? I look over at André Watson. He raises his arm and signals the drop goal. Everything is OK. We still have to deal with the kick-off but Trevor Woodman catches it and the ball is fed back to Catty to deliver the laziest yet most beautiful touch-kick in the history of English rugby. Then it's over. We've done it. My head is spinning like a tumble dryer. I jump up and down with Will Greenwood, shouting like a mad man, 'World Cup, World Cup'. In the emotion of the moment I am unable to come up with anything more profound. It does say it all, though – we are world champions.

As I stood there on the pitch afterwards, I was in shock. Nothing seemed to make sense. I couldn't reconcile the fact that I had been so low and then so high in the space of a few minutes. England had won the World Cup? That happened on television, to other teams, not to us. I felt out of place somehow and I didn't know what to do with myself.

Slowly, as we received the trophy and embarked on our exhausted, elated lap of honour in the rain, everything started to fall into place. I looked up at all the supporters around that magnificent stadium where I had suffered so after the Lions lost the series to the Wallabies in 2001 and finally felt at peace.

I can't say I enjoyed the match – there was too much riding on it. And with all the pressure I can't even say I enjoyed the tournament. But with a World Cup winners' medal around my neck, I did let myself enjoy that little walk around the pitch afterwards.

CELEB

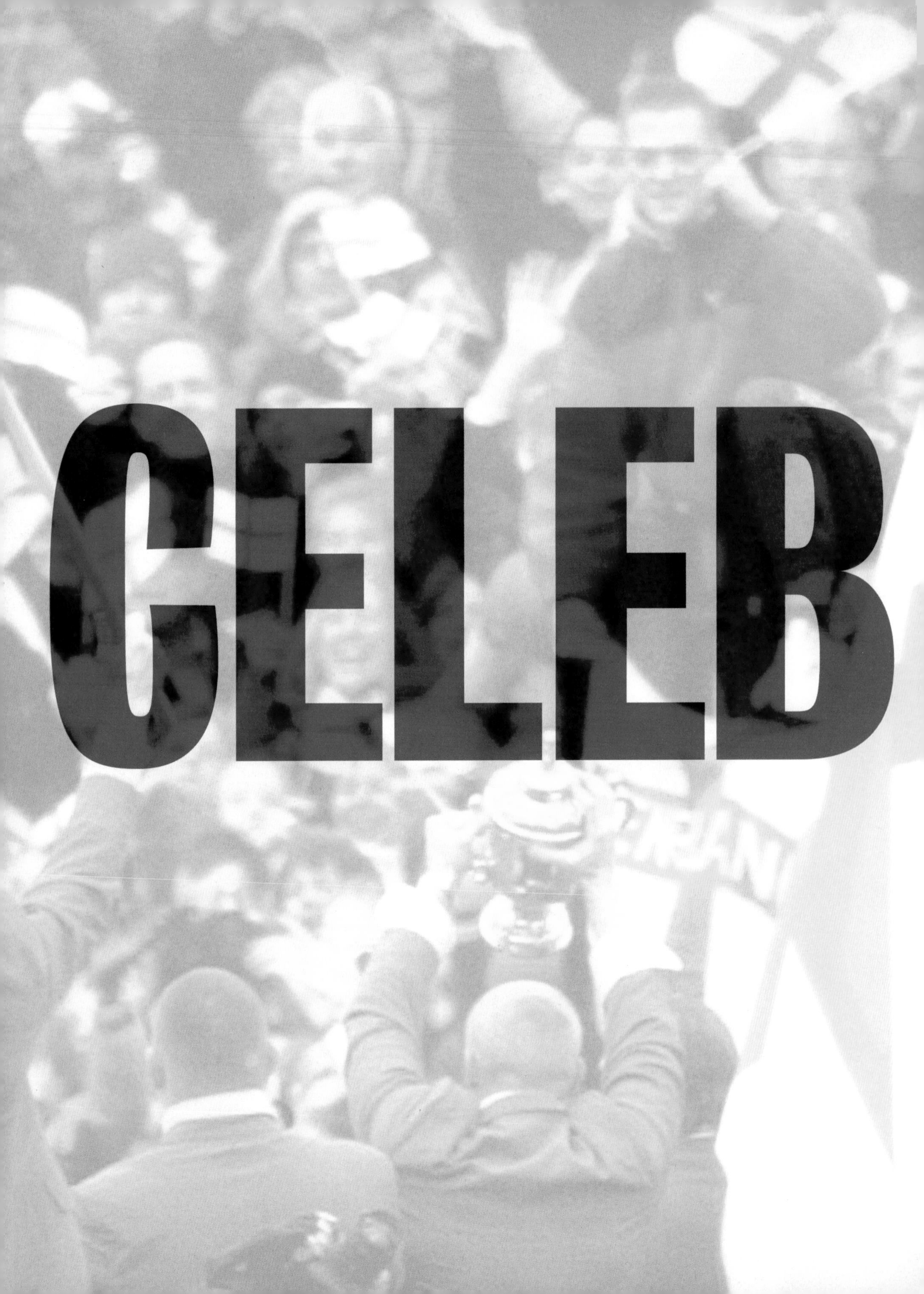

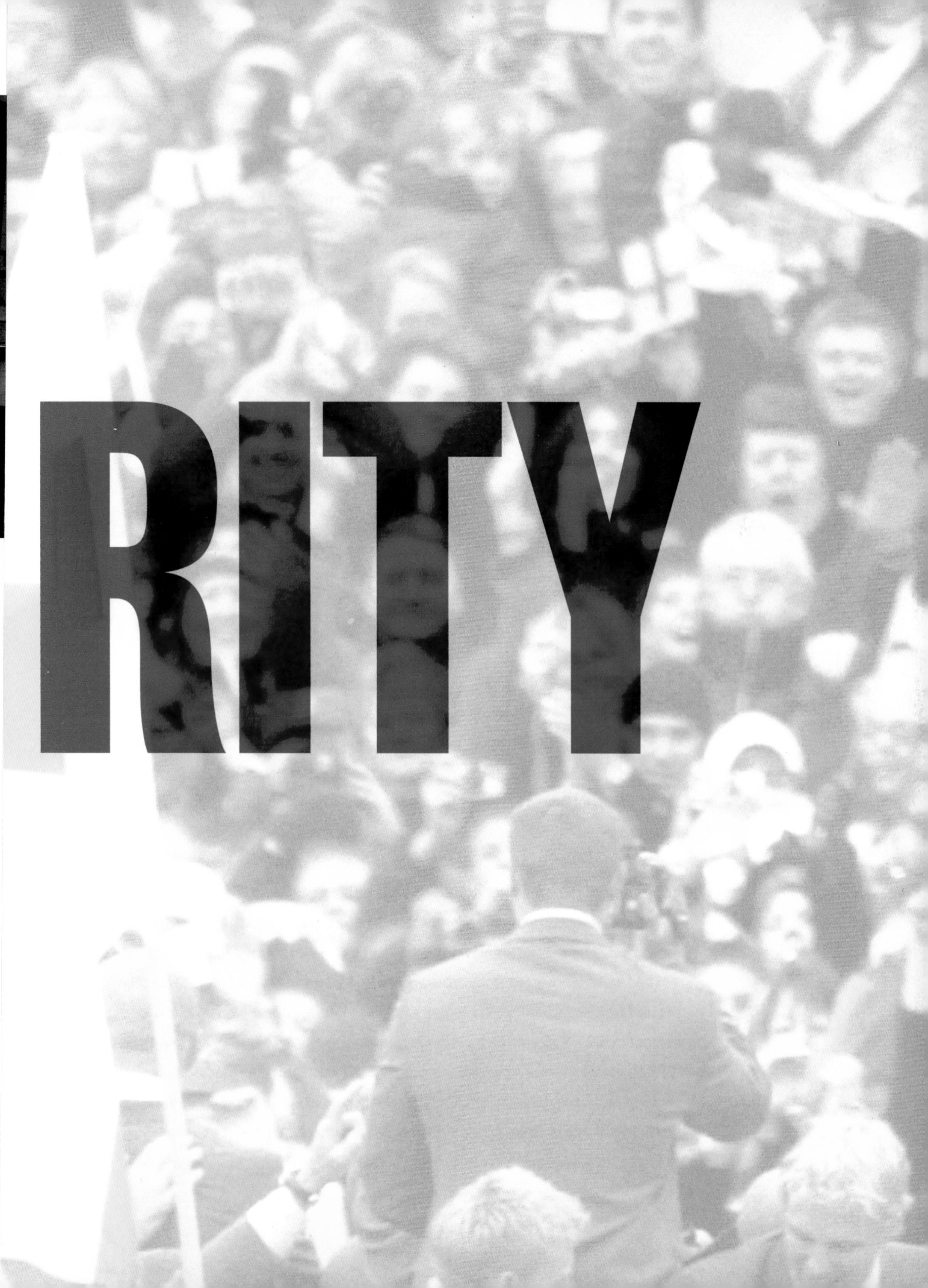
RITY

He congratulated us on our win, said we deserved it but that the Wallabies would be out to get us next time.

They did.

Others wrote to offer advice. I should smile more, said one; I should drive a British car rather than a Mercedes, read another. There was even a letter from a vicar saying that I should become a man of the cloth.

The letters came from places as far afield as Finland and Fiji, Malawi and Luxembourg; there were even a few from Australia – including one from Elton Flatley. He congratulated us on our win, said we deserved it but that the Wallabies would be out to get us next time. They did.

Many children wrote to say how they had started playing rugby after watching the World Cup which was gratifying, although one seven-year-old said he had been sent off for trying to tackle like me in a non-contact game. At the opposite end of the scale was a lovely note from an eighty-seven-year-old lady who was about to emigrate to South Africa a happy woman to 'pop her clogs' alongside her family.

It gradually began to dawn on me that the World Cup victory was an achievement that had crossed the boundaries between sports and gone beyond sport altogether. Somehow, by doing our jobs, we had touched people's lives. Wrapped up in the middle of our own little world in Australia we had had no conception of that. A common theme ran through much of the correspondence and it was extremely humbling. It was that we had inspired people and made them proud of their country, not only by winning but also, apparently, by how we had carried ourselves through the tournament. That made me want to go out and do it all over again.

If there was one event which illustrated the extent to which the country had been affected it was our victory parade. Looking at everyone from the top of the bus on that freezing December day was an incredible experience. It was an assault on the senses. Seeing three-quarters of a million people lining the streets of London and hearing the choruses of 'Swing Low' in Trafalgar Square was absolutely mad. If England won World Cups in major team sports more often it may have been different, but it had been a long wait since 1966.

The World Cup victory was an achievement that had gone beyond sport altogether. Somehow, by doing our jobs, we had touched people's lives.

I would probably have been more at ease watching than being watched but I tucked myself away as best I could at the back of the players' bus, next to my day-release partner Hilly, as we set off from the Inter Continental Hotel at Hyde Park Corner just before midday. The parade began properly at Marble Arch and it soon became obvious that we weren't going to be accompanied by tumbleweed down deserted streets as we had joked when the idea had first been suggested. The numbers just swelled and swelled and by the time the parade reached Oxford Circus it was a full-blown street party. We all looked down on it open-mouthed for the most part, exchanging comments of disbelief. All this for a rugby team?

A sea of smiling faces and a bottomless pit of warmth on the coldest of days

There was red and white confetti in the air and flags everywhere, there was even one up on the platform of a crane high in the sky. People were on top of bus shelters, clinging to lampposts, all yelling their support. One guy even climbed up a set of traffic lights to shake our hands. People hurled cameras up onto the bus for players to take pictures of each other. We then had to throw them back from thirty yards down the road as the bus moved on. They were all returned in one piece – apart from the ones Thommo threw!

As for the scenes in Trafalgar Square, they were amazing – a sea of smiling faces and a bottomless pit of warmth on the coldest of days. It was a country and a team saying thank you to each other. In amongst the faces was one very familiar one – my granddad. The police had let him through in front of the barrier so I could see and wave to him. It was an emotional moment for both of us. My grandma had passed away while I was in Australia.

The clamour and the euphoria were staggering, yet one of my clearest memories of it all is of turning off the procession route at the end and suddenly no-one being there. It was similar to the feeling after a match when you leave the ground, head home and close your front door behind you. Welcome back to real life. Except on this occasion, life became even more surreal afterwards. Hearing from the Queen how she had watched all bar one of the games, then visiting 10 Downing Street and finding the Prime Minister's son Leo in the England shirt he had worn throughout the tournament, brought home – if what we had just seen hadn't – how everyone had been caught up in the drama. No-one, it seemed, had been immune.

Some very important people had trodden those floors – a lot more important than the England rugby team

Tea and scones at Buckingham Palace was quite something. Inside it was just how you would imagine a fairytale palace would look. Everywhere there seemed to be masterpieces or wonderful sculptures. We were received in a suitably opulent room, dripping in chandeliers and with Rembrandts on the wall. I was quite taken with the history of it all. Some very important people had trodden those floors – a lot more important than the England rugby team. Drinking in all the tradition and splendour passed an edgy few minutes while we waited for the Queen. After what seemed an age the magnificent doors opened and in came – nine corgis. It was a slight anti-climax. Mark Regan whistled them over.

Eventually we did meet the Queen and posed with her for a picture with the trophy. She talked about how she had listened to the final on the radio and then watched the game on video later that evening. She said she was glad she didn't have to go through the tension of watching it live. I told her that she sounded like my mum who went shopping instead of watching the final. After she admitted she was in Tesco during extra time, the supermarket ran a full-page advert using a picture of her in some of the papers. The caption read: 'She shopped until he dropped.' Mum rarely watches me play. She just waits for the phone call from my dad afterwards to say I'm OK. I think she would prefer it if I played a non-contact sport like tennis.

The choreography was so exact; the whole performance had the feel of a complex backs' move

A few days later Mum was able to meet the Queen when I collected an MBE back at the Palace. The different categories of honours recipients were roped off from each other, giving the inside of one of the stateliest buildings in the world the look of a nightclub. We were strictly drilled on how to address the Queen and how to approach her to receive our honours. The choreography was so exact; the whole performance had the feel of a complex backs' move. Fortunately I didn't knock on.

The Queen has a definite aura about her. Obviously she was quite a lot smaller than a bunch of international rugby players but she had this presence which seemed to fill the room. Being used to life in the public eye, she asked me how I was coping with the attention. Prince William was at Buckingham Palace and we also chatted about life in the spotlight. It seemed to be a recurring theme. When we headed off to Downing Street, that was the topic with the Prime Minister too. Nice to know so many people care.

Walking through that famous black front door was a lot less like stepping into another world than entering Buckingham Palace. No 10 Downing Street is not your average house – it seems to go up and back an awful long way inside – but it is still a family home. There was a huge number of staff inside – you could hardly move for them all – and with the whole squad in there too it was quite crowded. Security was understandably an issue too. We were asked not to bring any unnecessary hand baggage and to leave cameras on the team bus.

I am genuinely embarrassed when people chant my name or crowd around me just because they have seen my face before on TV

It was the same at the Sports Personality of the Year awards. Here was a programme I had watched religiously with my family every year when I was growing up. So many legends had stood there, with that famous music playing at the end, holding the trophy with the camera on it. When my name was read out I felt like a fraud. Don't get me wrong, I was incredibly grateful to receive the award from Princess Anne, but when Johnno – the man who had led us to the World Cup – was standing behind me in second place it didn't feel right at all. I felt a lot happier accepting the team award. He deserved that individual award as much as anyone ever has in all the years I've been watching.

There was some criticism of the whole squad and the coaches being honoured in the New Year's list because of the numbers involved but I thought that was exactly right. It wasn't just the odd individual who had won the Webb Ellis Trophy.

As the goal-kicker and fly-half, I am always going to receive a lot of scrutiny – good and bad – but it does not equate to deserving it. I am genuinely embarrassed when people chant my name or crowd around me when I get off the bus just because they have seen my face before on TV as I line up a kick. I mean how can I look someone like Hilly in the eye and say I deserve it more than he does?

I didn't have women falling all over me when I was unknown so I don't see what should have changed just because of one drop-kick

I was able to laugh off some of the more ludicrous individual attention – the haircut of the year award, for instance. The Wilkinson 'look' was created by Ian Morrison at Salon 66 in Newcastle, a great bloke, chosen less for his international styling credentials than the fact that he has cut my Falcons team-mate Dave Walder's hair since he was four. Cost to the public, with wash, £11.50. I choose to have it cut at Ian's house to avoid the self-conscious, uncomfortable feelings that plague me when people stare in the barber's. The setting is hardly what you might imagine for an award-winning cut – the kitchen of a cosy house in Gosforth. You could not wish for a more down-to-earth backdrop. Dinner on the go, kids racing around pretending to be David Beckham, telly on in the next room – it is not a swanky King's Road hair artiste's. If I want my hair rinsed, I have to put my head in the sink with the washing-up.

Being voted the country's most fanciable male also amused me. The whole concept of being a pin-up does not fit in at all with the person I know I am. Although I'm learning to overcome my shyness, I'm still not that confident in social situations and I spend very little time on my appearance. I didn't have women falling all over me when I was unknown so I don't see what should have changed just because of one drop-kick. Who in their right minds would be interested in someone who spends most of his life booting an egg around muddy training pitches and the rest of it locked inside his house? If you're after lifestyle, I'm not really your man.

I could not simply shrug off other aspects of the outside world's interest in me. I found I could not go anywhere anonymously any more

However, I could not simply shrug off other aspects of the outside world's interest in me. I found I could not go anywhere anonymously any more.

Things were changing before the World Cup. The recognition rate was increasing at the same speed as rugby's popularity was growing. Even before the tournament I tried to avoid going to places where I knew there would be rugby supporters, but that was where I drew the line at altering the way I lived my life. I still more or less did what I wanted to do. I can't anymore. The World Cup's success in touching so many people has opened up millions more to the game, which is something I feel genuinely proud of. But it has also closed off just about every avenue for relaxation I had outside my own home. I used to enjoy shopping in Newcastle; now I wouldn't do it unless I had to. Visits to the cinema, a favourite release for me, are also a no-go unless very carefully planned. And this is Newcastle – the football hot-bed.

When I'm out I feel I can never really relax. When I was injured last season I went to watch Newcastle play at Leeds. It wasn't a cold day but I togged myself up in hat, scarf and coat so I could stand on the terraces behind the posts without anyone spotting me. Only one guy did and he asked for an autograph without drawing attention to me so there was no problem. But as I trailed away at the end of the game, staring at my feet so no-one would do that double-take look at me, I found myself feeling a little sensitive. Why should I have to go through all of this to watch a game of rugby with my dad?

I never asked
to be famous.
I just wanted
to play rugby

IF THERE WERE JUST ONE MAN AND A DOG WATCHING I WOULDN'T CARE I WOULD STILL PLAY THE GAME

When I play for England I understand I am public property. But when the rest of my life is opened up to comment and judgement that is a totally different scenario

I thought winning the World Cup was a good thing – why did it feel like we were being punished? I felt uptight, angry, depressed and vowed not to go near the sand again. But the pictures they had already taken appeared in three of the British tabloids which was like having our privacy invaded all over again.

It didn't stop when I returned home. I landed at Newcastle Airport to be confronted by another snapper who had his lens so close he ended up in the same section of the revolving door. He even had the cheek to ask me for another picture when my father and I had clearly told him that he was intruding. I used to read about people punching these characters and be astounded at how they could lose their cool so badly, but being on the other side of it I can understand their reaction now, if not condone it.

I don't know how these people can look at themselves in the mirror. The more intimate and private the moment, the more valuable it is to them and the more willing they are to intrude. These people find what they do acceptable, but I don't. I know everyone has to put bread on the table for their families but there are choices to be made in life. No-one is forced to do that job.

When I play for England, I understand I am public property. I know everything I do will be examined in pictures and words. That is absolutely fine. Everyone is entitled to their own opinion of me – whether I am playing well, whether I should be in the team – that's part of the deal. But when the rest of my life is opened up to comment and judgement that is a totally different scenario.

If all your existence amounts to is chasing fame for fame's sake, it is a life built on sand and is liable to come crashing down around you

Other sportsmen, like David Beckham, are better at handling the whole media circus. He deals with all the attention – positive and negative – fantastically, although not in a way I could ever manage. Accepting it will always be a part of his life, he is more pro-active and uses it to his advantage. I think you need a certain kind of outgoing personality to carry that off which I don't have. I have a group of very good sponsors but I try to represent them in the way I prepare, perform and behave on the rugby field, rather than by joining the celebrity circus.

I am very uneasy with the whole idea of a celebrity culture. Fame may be a spin-off of success in the sports and entertainment world, but if it turns your head you can lose sight of what helped you reach that position in the first place and then you have problems. Just because an actor gets his big break in a hit film, it doesn't mean he should ease off in his next role. If anything it should spur him on to give an even better performance. It's the same with sportsmen. Look at Beckham. He doesn't allow himself to be distracted despite all the madness around him. It is the core which is important, not all the peripheral flannel.

Not everyone recognises this and for some people their whole life appears to revolve around becoming a celebrity and then maintaining that status by increasingly desperate means. If all your existence amounts to is chasing fame for fame's sake, it is a life built on sand and is liable to come crashing down around you. It is short term and empty and certainly not the life for me.

INTEG

RITY

'Every man's work is always a portrait of himself'

Samuel Butler

I have been accused of being an obsessive. I used to shy away from that description because of its connotations – someone kindly described me as a 'basket case' at the World Cup. However, in the case of training, at least, I feel more comfortable with the term now.

When I go out onto the pitch I want to look at my opposite number and feel as if I am stronger, quicker and better than he is. I need to believe that whatever he throws at me I will be more than equal to it. For that to happen, I have to prepare obsessively.

I don't view the sacrifices I make as a pain. They are my choice. Once I get something in my head that I need to give up or change, after the initial battle to forgo it, I will forget about it completely. If something does not help improve me as a rugby player, I'll bin it. Simple as that.

I don't drink alcohol. I used to indulge in the odd binge to let the lid off the pressure cooker but gradually the gaps between the big nights out grew and grew until I stopped drinking altogether. I no longer feel it is part of me. Although we all probably deserved one, I didn't even have a tipple the night we won the World Cup. Instead I drank a couple of Diet Cokes as we celebrated in a nightclub in The Rocks. The last time I touched alcohol was when England beat Australia in Melbourne in June 2003.

I eat healthily. All the benefits of a hard training session can be lost by munching the wrong food afterwards so I choose not to eat sweets, biscuits or chocolate. People have given up buying me Easter eggs because I just pass them on. I have a real complex about giving in to this sort of temptation – even if I took a single bite, which would have no consequence whatsoever for my fitness, I would feel guilty and regard it as mental weakness on my part. There is that obsessive streak again.

I also steer clear of fast food. In fact I have taken its avoidance to a new level. I refuse to go into a fast-food outlet – to use the toilet even – in case anyone got the wrong idea and thought I was sneaking in a quick burger.

England have a nutritionist, Adam Carey, who provides dietary advice and keeps me up to speed with what I should and shouldn't be eating. He also recommends the supplements I take, a necessary part of professional rugby life if not always the easiest to stomach. I love good food but it has to be healthy.

As for smoking, it is my pet hate – it always has been. When I was younger I used to have nightmares that someone was pinning me down and forcing me to smoke. I would wake up feeling like something was terribly wrong, only to realise I had been dreaming and my non-smoking record was still intact. I don't ever want to smoke a cigarette.

When a fast-food chain approached me after the World Cup to endorse their product, I turned them down – it would have been hypocritical

I try to be consistent. Because I don't drink and try not to eat unhealthy food, I would never tell others to do so. When a fast-food chain approached me after the World Cup to endorse their product, I turned them down. I hadn't been in one of their outlets since I became a professional rugby player – it doesn't fit with the lifestyle – so it would have been hypocritical. A snack-food company also approached me but, again, it wasn't a product I would eat myself or encourage prospective sportsmen to eat so I said no.

People tell me I am in the position of being a role model to young people so I want to provide a good example. If I have achieved a position of influence, then I want to use that power wisely. I remember walking into the Newcastle changing room as an eighteen-year-old and seeing legends like Inga Tuigamala and Pat Lam. I instinctively gravitated to them and the way they went about things. Fortunately they were great examples of how to live your life. Inga talked in great detail about

If young people are looking up to me, they are looking up to the genuine me, not a fake. The way I live cannot be an act

using his time playing rugby to build his reputation as a person and player. He told me that will be all that is left when the boots are hung up.

I want to make sure that if young people are looking up to me, they are looking up to the genuine me, not a fake. The way I live cannot be an act. Image is a buzz word of our times and central to the celebrity culture which prevails at the moment but the only image you can truly portray without fear of being exposed is that of the person you are.

I am not, in the practising sense of the word, religious. My parents are not really churchgoers so I wasn't brought up that way but they did give me, through my upbringing, the means of determining my own black and white picture of wrong and right. I'm not quite sure where I stand on organised religion but I like to believe

I live my life as if a twenty-four-hour surveillance camera is trained on me. At the end of my days, I want to be able to hand over and sign away the video

in judgement from a greater power. I live my life as if a twenty-four-hour surveillance camera is trained on me, which is ironic as lately it has felt as if one has been. At the end of my days, I want to be able to hand over and sign away the video, happy that its contents accurately reflect the person I am.

There are boundaries which I set for myself and do not want to cross. I won't take my clothes off for pictures, for instance. My reticence is partly to do with appearances. I don't find images of people without their clothes on all that attractive – I prefer to leave something to the imagination because mystery is a very appealing part of a person. But it is also to try to preserve what remains of my privacy. I don't want everyone else owning all of me. During the World Cup, England spent some time at a water park relaxing. I'd have liked to join in but there were photographers waiting to snap the players without their shirts on. I kept my top on and watched instead – so did Jason Robinson. We both found the idea of being picked off half-naked by the snappers a bit grubby. I did take my top off for a picture once when I was very young for a health magazine. I had my arm twisted after forty minutes of trying to say no. It is something I learned from but still resent very strongly.

None of us is perfect. I can be grumpy and fractious to the people I care for the most, particularly before matches. If I'm not training well, I am not the best person to be around. There are times when I become too obsessed with trivialities and fall below the standards I set myself but that should not stop me trying to reach them.

You give a part of yourself away when you take money off people and I want to feel happy with where that part of me is going

After the World Cup I also rejected an approach to take part in coffee adverts – I don't drink the stuff – and a spread in *Hello!* magazine. A million pounds or not, that was a non-starter. After working so hard protecting what little privacy I had left, the last thing I wanted was to invite a photographer in to show the world my 'tastefully decorated' bathroom.

Aside from the promotional work I was committed to with my five existing sponsors, I said no to virtually every commercial opportunity or public appearance after the World Cup. I thought it would be seen as cashing in.

I don't want to come across as some sort of martyr. I earn a good living in a wonderful job so I am in the fortunate position of being able to pick and choose what I do. I don't judge others for making their own decisions over what constitutes a reasonable offer. It's just that you give a part of yourself away when you take money off people and I want to feel happy with where that part of me is going. I feel I've been very lucky with the companies that have taken an interest in me.

That's not to say there weren't some corking offers. The chance to be immortalised inside a glass paperweight or to feature on a pair of tiny rubber boots attached to a key ring was tempting. But not that tempting. The ideas for Wilkinson board games, pens and models were no-nos too, especially as the dolls didn't even look like me. There was one strange grog-like figure, which bore a closer resemblance to Jude Law, and a hand-made plaster sculpture of me whose head unfortunately fell off.

I was inundated with requests from charities, which meant having to make some difficult decisions over which I felt I could support. Raffling off one of my World Cup final shirts was a practical way of doing so once I had made my mind up. I chose the raffle ticket idea because I didn't want it simply to go to the highest bidder at an auction, as is usually the way with sports memorabilia. I wanted to give fans the chance to win it.

I try not to short-change anyone. When I'm conducting a kicking clinic I will always give more time to the kids who are there than I promised. A chain of frustrated parents who have waited shivering on the touchline will confirm that what is supposed to be an hour's session usually snowballs into something longer. It does when I'm on my own so I might as well give them the authentic experience! Besides, it is a professional duty not to mess with the dreams and ambitions of someone who is there to learn. I know how disappointing bad teaching can be. One of the team's sponsors in Australia threw a golf day and after finishing my kicking, I turned up late but excited about the prospect of a golf lesson. I live right next to a course and play occasionally so I was keen to iron out one or two of my long list of faults. The instructor took a little time out to just confuse me and then walked away. It was the perfect example of how to discourage someone from ever picking up a golf club again. The worst thing was that I was really looking forward to it, even if he wasn't. It is a useful reference point for me for when the boot is on the other foot. The experience the children have may well contribute to whether they stick with rugby or not.

If I do promotional work, I will always catch up the time on the training field, even if it means an evening kicking session alone on my local football pitch. I kick six days a week. How long for depends on how well a session goes. The minimum is probably an hour and a quarter, the maximum — well, there is no maximum. I am trying to taper down some of the kicking to give my life more balance but I am finding this very difficult.

I sometimes become frustrated that others do not share my all-consuming approach to my sport. I can't rest until I have tamed the devil in my head and if that means kicking until all hours, then it just has to be done.

I earn a good living in a wonderful job so I am in the fortunate position of being able to pick and choose what I do

Some people have observed that my approach would be ideally suited to an individual sport. However, a crucial part of what drives me to go that extra mile is a reluctance to let down my team-mates

I complete each session with six kicks at goal from different positions. I have to make every one before I can go home. If I don't, the sequence starts again. My conscience doesn't allow me to stop before the set is complete. My record, and it is not one I'm particularly proud of, stands at five hours, set when I was seventeen.

I have come to realise, however, that my way is not for everyone. Not only is it weird to keep going for that long but I know now it can also be counter-productive. There's nothing I can do to stop myself but I do at least recognise the danger. The point of all the hours on the training pitch is to enable me to feel satisfied. Other players can manage that with half the effort. For me, it just wouldn't work. Understanding this was a huge step forward for me.

The one person I take notice of when he tells me I am overdoing it is Blackie. Well, usually. Sometimes I will slip in a crafty kicking session while he's not looking.

I might kick with my brother or one of the Newcastle Academy lads and occasionally Rob Andrew will appear out of his office to re-live his distant youth and kick the balls back. For quite a lot of the time, though, I train alone at Kingston Park. I think having to go and fetch the stray balls that have bounced into the stand in order to repeat the exercise adds mental toughness.

If you were to come along to watch, you would hear me talking to myself as I go along. More persuasive evidence to back the basket-case argument on the surface, but there is a sane point to the cries of 'sweet', 'great kick – that's the one', 'concentrate – hard foot' and 'if I do that again I'm going to punch myself'. In technical jargon this is called self-talk. I use it in matches to re-enforce my

I can't rest until I have tamed the devil in my head and if that means kicking until all hours, then it just has to be done

If I'm telling
myself I'm
doing well,
it will help me
to do so

confidence. If I'm telling myself I'm doing well, it will help me to do so. Telling myself that it's not so good is also important as long as the criticism is underpinned with technical coaching to help correct the next one.

I like to compare the perfect kick to a jigsaw puzzle. Every time I am away from the training ground, the box the jigsaw is in is shaken up, so when I go back to kick the next day it doesn't quite fit together any more. The aim of every session is to reassemble those pieces to make the complete picture again.

I didn't understand the mechanics of how to do so until I started working with Dave Alred when I was sixteen. He was Rob's kicking coach at the time. The beauty with Dave was that he was able to call on all sorts of influences from a varied playing career which incorporated both codes of rugby and American football. He basically ripped apart my technique and reconstructed it so that as many of the variable elements as possible were taken out. It was difficult for me at first but as I practised I could see the improvement with my own eyes. The most important thing Dave has taught me is how to be my own coach. I know I will make mistakes but I also know why, so I can put things right.

There are probably people who look at my kicking stance now and think it must be uncomfortable, what with my hands cupped in front of me. Exactly the opposite is true. This is the position in which I feel at ease, shielded against all distractions. It has evolved over many seasons.

When I kick I try to blot out the outside world by employing a yoga technique. It is called centring and involves channelling all my inner energy from a core point behind my navel. As I prepare to strike the ball, I concentrate on the energy surging down my left leg and into my left foot. This creates an explosive contact with the ball. That is the theory anyway.

Subconsciously, as I worked on doing this, my hands took up their prayer position. When I started out they were a lot further apart but the style has changed over the years until it has become something of a calling card. I even had it trademarked after the World Cup. Not everyone warms to it. The cupped hands were voted the most irritating sporting trait in the world, ahead of Tim Henman's clenched fist, in one magazine. But it works for me, so I'll stick with it.

The cupped hands were voted the most irritating sporting trait in the world. But it works for me, so I'll stick with it

Oddly, my hands remain apart if I use my right foot to kick at goal. I do this in practice sometimes as it helps with the drop-kicking. When I was sixteen I used to take goal-kicks in matches with both feet, using my right from the left-hand side of the pitch and vice versa. I gave that up when I realised how much time would be needed to perfect the art with just one foot. However, I stuck with the two-footed approach with the punting and the drop-kicking.

Maybe my way of doing things comes from having a dad who was left-footed and an elder brother who preferred his right. As a right-handed five-year-old I used to find it an interesting challenge to try to pass a ball equally as well off my left hand. It was the same the opposite way round with kicking. A lot was made during the World Cup of me targeting the unfortunate Doris behind the posts in kicking practice, an imaginary lady holding a copy of *The Times*. It's nothing personal. It is just a means of narrowing down the zone I'm aiming for. So if I'm slightly off, the ball should still go through the middle of the posts. Doris came into my life in 1998, in the week leading up to the Test against Australia. I was struggling badly to hit through the new Summit rugby balls and nothing I tried seemed to help. Eventually Dave suggested we forget about technique and imagine trying to hit an empty seat in the stand behind the posts. As we narrowed the margin of error the seat became a lady (Dave's idea), then the target became her newspaper and finally her ice cream. It really helped me with my confidence and accuracy. Being a kicker obviously involves extra practice compared to the rest of the team but I try to do more fitness work too. When it comes to conditioning, there is no escape from the basics of running and lifting weights but I try to train more efficiently and often in a different way to other players to gain an edge. There are so many good young players coming through that to stay still I have to keep moving ahead.

I trust Blackie's guidance in this area implicitly. From day to day I never know what he has in store for me. I have turned up for sessions and found badminton and short tennis rackets waiting for me. My elder brother Mark, who is also a professional at Newcastle, is my usual training partner but Blackie has provided everyone from karting drivers to a Hollywood actor who was filming in the north-east, all with the idea of keeping training fresh and interesting. The programme

changes each session and my challenge is to react positively to whatever he throws in front of me and be ready to give everything I have.

If you peered into the breeze-block gym under the West Stand at Kingston Park, with its weights machines and running track, you would be as likely to find me with a football or a punchbag as a rugby ball. Like Dave Alred, Blackie is a man of many parts, having trained Newcastle United in the past and been a professional boxer, and he imparts the knowledge and self-confidence he has accumulated in these fields.

The boxing is not designed to help me in the event of a fight on the field, but it is incredible for explosive power and fitness. The punching can also replicate a strong hand-off and the footwork is useful for getting myself in the right position for a tackle. The spin-off of regularly pummelling a punchball or a drunken sailor is that I could probably hold my own in a boxing ring, although wild horses couldn't drag me into one.

Equally, the point of the football work is not to stop me looking like a fool in adverts with David Beckham or to recall my glory days in the Farnham Town under-elevens defence, but to work on co-ordination and concentration. Blackie will often demand a football skill, like continuously volleying a ball against a wall without it touching the floor, when I am already dripping in sweat from my exertions. The act of performing a precise skill under extreme stress simulates what happens in every rugby match, even if at Twickenham I rarely flick a rugby ball onto the back of my neck and balance it there.

I use a lot of football training techniques because footballers generally use their feet and evasive skills more often than rugby players. When I set about improving my footwork a few seasons ago, Blackie used drills Kevin Keegan had employed as a player to spin off defenders. Blackie tells me there was no-one better. You learn from the best, whichever sport they happen to play, and I do like football. I suppose I am an adopted Newcastle United fan these days but I have a soft spot for Norwich City. My granddad, Phil Wilkinson, has a season ticket and used to take my brother and me to Carrow Road for Boxing Day fixtures.

> I could probably hold my own in a boxing ring, although wild horses couldn't drag me into one

The act of
performing a
precise skill
under extreme
stress simulates
what happens in
every rugby
match, even if
at Twickenham I
will rarely flick
a rugby ball
onto the back
of my neck and
balance it there

The sessions with Blackie, which can last a couple of hours, are extremely intense. The exercises are sharp and there are few breaks. Although England's pre-World Cup training was tough, I had endured worse before with Blackie. I have got to the stage where flogging myself is second nature. I wouldn't say I relish the thought of training but it is something I know I have to do and I also know how good it will feel afterwards. The thought that I have moved myself on is a comforting one. I gain a perverse kick out of the agony I am putting myself through. I train to the point where my shirt is drenched, my body is screaming at me and I feel like I'm going to be sick. I often have to lie flat out to recover because I feel light-headed and dizzy. The secret of dealing with the pain is not to look to the end of the exercise but to concentrate on what you are doing at that precise moment. If you let your mind think of the torture ahead it will try to persuade you that you cannot face it.

Blackie keeps a benevolent eye on what I am doing, occasionally barking out instructions, but always encouraging me rather than chastising me. He takes a lot of time to befriend and get to know well every member of the Newcastle squad, assessing their physical and mental strengths, limits and weaknesses. He knows me inside out so he does not ask me to carry out a specific number of repetitions or spell out how long I should work for; he just keeps me going until he decides I have endured enough. This is incredible for mental toughness. It is

I wouldn't say I relish the thought of training but it is something I know I have to do and I also know how good it will feel afterwards

I train to the point where my shirt is drenched, my body is screaming at me and I feel like I'm going to be sick

impossible to save yourself for the latter part of a session if you haven't a clue what you will be doing or for how long. The only answer is to go at it hammer and tongs from the start.

There has only been one occasion when I have failed a test he has set me. It was at the gym at his house and the challenge was to complete a session consisting of a nasty set of exercises on a cross-aerobic system. Only four members of the Newcastle squad had managed it but because I was one of them I expected to be able to do so again. When I didn't, I was livid. I had been ill the previous week but I refused to recognise this as the reason why I had failed and I was so upset I stormed out, roaring in frustration, past this startled bloke waiting outside to use the gym, and kicked Blackie's garage doors. The bloke turned out to be Paul Gascoigne.

Some people have observed that my approach would be ideally suited to an individual sport. It is something I have considered myself. However, a crucial part of what drives me to go that extra mile is a reluctance to let down my team-mates. You have to have more to lose than just the game.

If I have achieved certain standards then they have every right to expect me to reach them in every game I play. If you play well one week for England and put in the big tackles, your club colleagues have every right to expect you to match those standards the next time you play for your club.

I have no respect for players who do not prepare to give their all every game and those who pick and choose the matches to peak in. If an individual only puts maximum effort in for his country and cruises through run-of-the-mill club games, he needs to examine his integrity. There is no such thing as a great England player and an average club player. He is just an average player with a poor attitude.

We are all well paid and we owe it to our team-mates, fans and families to commit everything totally in every game. It is inexcusable not to. It means you are not a team man – and in my book there are few more powerful insults in rugby than that.

I don't deny that a lot of what I do, I do for myself. All the practice is aimed at self-improvement. But part of that is a desire to show my team-mates what I am capable of and, if possible, to surprise and please them. If I flatten someone in a tackle and hear one of my colleagues chuckle at the outcome, as has happened once or twice, then the thrill of doing so is heightened.

It just isn't in my make-up. When I clatter someone with a heavy tackle I like to see them go down quickly but I don't like to see them stay down. There is no satisfaction in injuring an opponent. If you tackle with the correct technique there is no reason why anyone should end up hurt – you or the guy who ends up on the floor. What I don't like to see is the sort of cowardly stiff-arm tackle which you can do nothing to protect yourself from and which can end someone's game or career. That is a disgrace.

With all the cameras that are around at professional matches these days, the dirty player has all but disappeared. Those that do indulge generally use cheap shots to try to put opponents off their games rather than hurt them. It is the same idea with sledging. The bulk of the exchanges on the field are good-humoured but there are one or two characters who like to dish out the verbals.

I never quite managed to crack the art of sledging – I only ever got myself into awkward situations through being cocky. Breaking into the Newcastle side as an eighteen-year-old gave me a higher opinion of myself than I should have had and I basically tended to get a little over-excited, telling opponents how well I thought I was doing or how badly they were faring.

I remember Rob Andrew getting involved in some pushing and shoving in one match against London Scottish while Newcastle were scoring a try, and I came over to offer my wisdom. 'No, no, stop this – you go and stand under the posts while I kick this one over,' I said. After delivering my knockout line, I suddenly realised the try had been scored in the corner and that there was a fair chance of me looking even more of an idiot by missing. As it was, the conversion went over even but there was certainly no crowing on my part. I was just relieved to have saved face after putting myself under a whole load of unnecessary extra pressure. I decided after this incident to quit while I was ahead.

I have grown up since then and I now limit the verbals to geeing up my own side or occasionally acknowledging an opponent for a good kick or a big hit on me. If I have any breath left.

Your heart is pounding like a hammer, your mouth as dry as a desert, your stomach knotted with nerves. You are willing to put your body on the line for your comrades, to do whatever it takes to achieve victory

HE

ROES

'Genius is one per cent inspiration and ninety-nine per cent perspiration'

Thomas Edison

Everyone has heroes. As a sports-mad kid, it was natural that mine would be sportsmen. Being a great ambassador and humble person is all very well but when you are growing up those aren't the main pre-requisites for choosing your idols. The common link between the individuals who fascinated me was that they were winners – not only that, but they dominated their sports to a staggering extent. Despite the fact that they were all performing in incredibly competitive environments against many other great athletes, they still managed to stand head and shoulders above everyone else. I didn't know then, but I understand now, how much toil that must have taken. All the talent in the world will get you nowhere without blood, sweat and tears. These guys had class but they welded a ferocious work ethic to their natural ability.

WALTER PAYTON

Channel 4 introduced a whole new sporting world into the Wilkinson sitting room in the 80s with their coverage of American football. I was fascinated. This strange sport from across the Atlantic seemed to have everything – power, pace, spectacular collisions and, above all, Walter Payton. The dynamic Chicago Bears running back used to light up my Sunday evenings. He seemed to spend every weekend defying gravity to leap over defences or run straight through them for improbable touchdowns. I was head of his Farnham fan club. While everyone else sported their football tops, I used to wear this white T-shirt with his name ironed on in black felt letters.

Payton held the NFL's rushing record for eighteen years. He broke it in 1984 and when he retired after the 1987 season he had extended it to 16,726 yards. That's almost ten miles through some seriously heavy traffic. They called him Sweetness but there wasn't much sweet about running into him. He was 5ft 10in of pure power. He wasn't the quickest running back around but he was incredibly destructive. 'If I'm going to get hit,' he once said, 'why let the guy who's going to hit me get the best shot? I explode into the guy who's trying to tackle me.' He talked about beating the opponent to the hit, a statement that has made many an appearance on my game-day preparation sheets in both attack and defence. It wasn't all a case of bang, crash, wallop, though – his footwork was fantastic too. What a centre he would have made if he had been introduced to rugby instead of gridiron.

Despite all the contact, he only missed one game in thirteen seasons for the Bears, which is an incredible record of durability in a sport like American football. And he wasn't just consistent, he was consistently brilliant. Between 1976 and 1980 he led the league's rushing stats every year. He was part of the famous side that won the Superbowl in 1985 and was held in such high esteem by the Bears that when he retired they retired his No. 34 jersey as well. Sadly, he died in 1999 at the age of just forty-five.

American football holds a fascination for quite a few rugby players – Martin Johnson is another big fan. As a self-confessed statto, he,

He seemed to spend every weekend defying gravity to leap over defences or run straight through them for improbable touchdowns

I can see a day when the USA make it to the top table of world rugby

along with my brother, is my information source for anything I want to know about the game.

The sports are close cousins with their base blocks of running, passing, tackling and kicking. Clive went over to the States soon after taking over as England coach to study the setup at the Denver Broncos. Their model of specialist coaches for all areas of the game was one he transplanted successfully into rugby. I use an American football in practice sometimes. It is harder to kick than a rugby ball because it has a smaller sweet spot, so I know if I am punting that well then it should be easier when it comes to the day job. But while I enjoy knocking a ball about with my brother and watching gridiron, I'm not sure I would want to play it professionally. The specialist nature of the sport means that a kicker – which is what I would presumably be – does not get to take part in the other areas of the game and without the running and tackling I'm sure I would end up frustrated. The only time the kicker gets to throw his weight around is on a punt return and most of them seem to keep out of the way when it comes to tackling. A notable exception, whose example I think I'd have to follow, would be Darren Bennett of the Minnesota Vikings. Mind you, he is 6ft 5in and 17st and a former Aussie Rules footballer.

I can see a day when the USA make it to the top table of world rugby – the Eagles gave a glimpse of their potential at the World Cup. They beat Japan and gave Scotland a scare with one of the biggest packs at the tournament. And they pushed a good French side to the limit in Connecticut in the summer, losing 39-31 after leading the Six Nations champions at half time. The sky is the limit for them if they can persuade some of those gridiron guys to get rid of the helmets and padding. Even if rugby just took the unsuccessful NFL guys, the USA would be some force.

MICHAEL JORDAN

Basketball may not be all that big this side of the Atlantic but the one American player every British sports fan will have heard of is Michael Jordan. His performances transcended any cultural divide.

Whenever I watched an NBA match, it seemed pre-ordained that the following script prevailed: a see-saw match goes into the final few seconds with one score between the teams. Everything hangs on the last play. The ball finds its way to Michael Jordan who has one shot to pull the game out of the fire. He makes it. Every time. I can't think of any sportsman who has struck so many significant shots under pressure. In rugby terms, he would be the man to make the kick from the corner to win the game. Only he would do it every week. There was his hanging jump shot which decided the 1989 playoff for the Chicago Bulls against the Cleveland Cavaliers. And then there was his three-pointer with just twenty-five seconds left on the clock that won the 1997 finals.

He would pull it all off with such style; he seemed to find basketball so easy. In fact, when he had mastered it, he briefly turned his hand to baseball to challenge himself in another environment. The flirtation did not last long and he returned to basketball to continue his domination of the sport. His record speaks for itself – five times the NBA's most valuable player, the leading scorer in the league ten times and the star of a Bulls side which won the championship six times. In his eleven full seasons with the Bulls he was top scorer ten times, averaging over thirty points per game. It may have been his showmanship which amazed everyone but he backed the flash stuff up with results. He would graft as hard as anyone for the team in defence.

I have Michael Jordan's autograph. This is a scandalous piece of name-dropping, but it was Daley Thompson who obtained it for me. Daley was another performer who left clear water between himself and the rest of his sport but, more importantly, he is also a friend of my manager, Tim Buttimore. Tim asked Daley to beg, borrow or steal Jordan's signature and he did. So, thanks to one of the greatest athletes Britain has produced, I have a personally signed photo of perhaps the greatest athlete in history. It is addressed to Johnny with an 'H'. You can't have everything.

> I can't think of any sportsman who has struck so many significant shots under pressure

BORIS BECKER

It is one of my great regrets that I never saw Boris Becker play at Wimbledon. I used to go along with my mum every year but we only ever had tickets for the outside courts. And Becker was a man destined for the show courts.

He was always centre stage, right from the time he swept through the tournament to become the youngest winner in 1985 as an incredibly powerful seventeen-year-old. He was still at school at the time. He must have been remarkably mature, physically and mentally, to beat the best players in the world at such a tender age.

He is on record as saying he found instant fame difficult to cope with – something I can relate to – but he had the sort of personality which seemed to enable him to grow as a player when the spotlight was on him. Like Andre Agassi, I suppose. He just seemed to have this swagger which told everyone else he wasn't afraid of them. They might have been older but they weren't better. The tennis world must have wondered what had hit it when this big German arrived on the scene. Becker went on to win two more Wimbledon singles titles in 1986 and 1989 and overall reached the final six times in seven years – an incredible record.

> He just seemed to have this swagger which told everyone else he wasn't afraid of them

As well as being a precocious talent, Becker was a great entertainer who people really warmed to. He was self-assured – on the brink of cocky – but he had the talent to carry it off. I remember him creaming a return past David Weaton in the 1991 semi-final to win the match in straight sets at Wimbledon. Before the ball had even passed Weaton on his way to the net, Becker was walking forward, hand held high in triumph.

I can't help loving that sort of stuff. I have a basketball video at home featuring Larry Bird, the Boston Celtics legend, in a shoot-out contest. With the clock running down fast Bird, who up to that point had struggled, needs the last four balls from the corner – the toughest part of the court – to beat his rivals. The first hits the target, quick as you like, and as he launches the fourth ball, with two and three still in the air, Bird knows straight away he's made the pressure shot. He just strolls away with his finger in the air. Sure enough, plop. Straight into the back of the

League was ahead of union as a game when I was growing up. It seemed to have so much more flair than union, which was very dependent on the conditions and over-technical by comparison

Hanley was renowned as a consummate professional and what I loved about him was that, having reached the top in this country, he didn't just sit back and take the easy option, he pushed himself even further by taking on the challenge of playing in Australia. He won their respect, taking Balmain Tigers to a grand final in 1988 and in the same year led Great Britain to a 26-12 win over the Kangaroos in Sydney – the last time we won in Australia. The Australians were a big influence on English rugby league, and on me too. I enjoyed watching creative half-backs like Ricky Stuart and Brad Fittler, as well as the power players such as Mal Meninga, Steve Menzies and Steve Renouf. With talent like that, it's no wonder Great Britain have generally struggled against the Kangaroos in Ashes series.

League was ahead of union as a game when I was growing up. It seemed to have so much more flair than union, which was very dependent on the conditions and over-technical by comparison.

Times have changed now, with some of the best league players like Jason Robinson and Henry Paul switching codes in Britain, and Sailor, Rogers and Tuqiri playing union for the Wallabies. But even stripped of some of its assets, I still like league and watch more of it than union on television. I don't necessarily find it a better game any more but I do find it more relaxing viewing. Tuning into a union match, however gripping, can seem like a busman's holiday. I end up analysing the play rather than enjoying the action.

I've always said I would love to try league – following in the footsteps of someone like Jonathan Davies would be quite a challenge – but as I go further down the union path it becomes less and less likely. Not many players go from union to league now both are professional.

Music has grown to play an increasingly important role in my life

Perhaps this is why, outside sport, Arnold Schwarzenegger was my hero growing up. As a kid who was fairly small for my age I was keen on the idea of growing big and strong and no-one seemed to be bigger and stronger than Arnie. I wasn't particularly fixated with his acting – although when I gave up counting, I had seen the film *Predator* thirty-seven times – it was his power. He had muscles on muscles and won seven Mr Universe titles. He might not have been Sir Ralph Richardson but he could deliver a line, which will probably come in handy in his political career now that he is Governor of California.

I never really had rock heroes but music was always there in the background at home and it has grown to play an increasingly important role in my life. The first band to make an impression on me was The Beatles. They were what my parents listened to and I picked up on the genius of John Lennon because of them. Later, I got into bands like The Verve and Coldplay in a big way too. I'd like to meet Chris Martin.

However, if there is one musician I would have at my fictional dinner party it would be Noel Gallagher. Obviously I would need to stock up on the alcohol first. Oasis have provided the soundtrack to a lot of my adult life. 'Wonderwall' was the song I sang (badly) on the team bus after my England debut to continue the tradition of all first caps and it was also the first tune I learned on the guitar. As for 'Married With Children', well, that song played a part in England beating New Zealand in Wellington ahead of the World Cup.

I had been learning it on the guitar on that trip and for some reason I couldn't get it out of my head. Everywhere I went the song came with me, including onto the pitch that night. I was even humming it in my mind as I went through my goal-kicking routine. It is odd the way you can react to these pressurised situations. I had become so fixated with the song that my brain wouldn't let me take a kick until I had finished the chorus. Each time I lined up a penalty, I had to wait at the end of my run-up until I had completed it in my head. The kicks probably took longer than usual but the process helped to relax me. On a windy night at the Westpac Stadium I kicked four out of five, plus a drop goal. The song finishes with the words 'Goodbye. I'm going home'. England went home happy. We won 15-13.

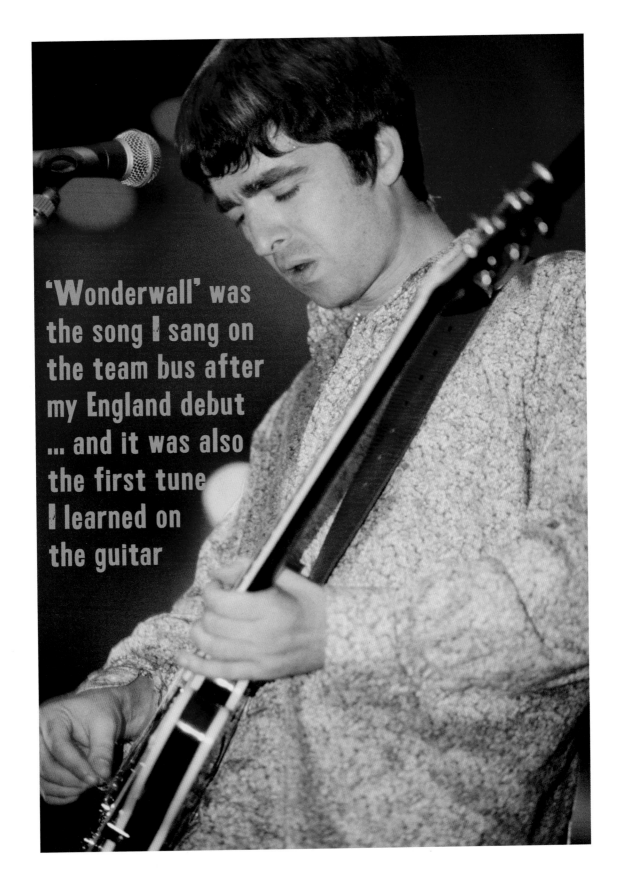

'Wonderwall' was the song I sang on the team bus after my England debut ... and it was also the first tune I learned on the guitar

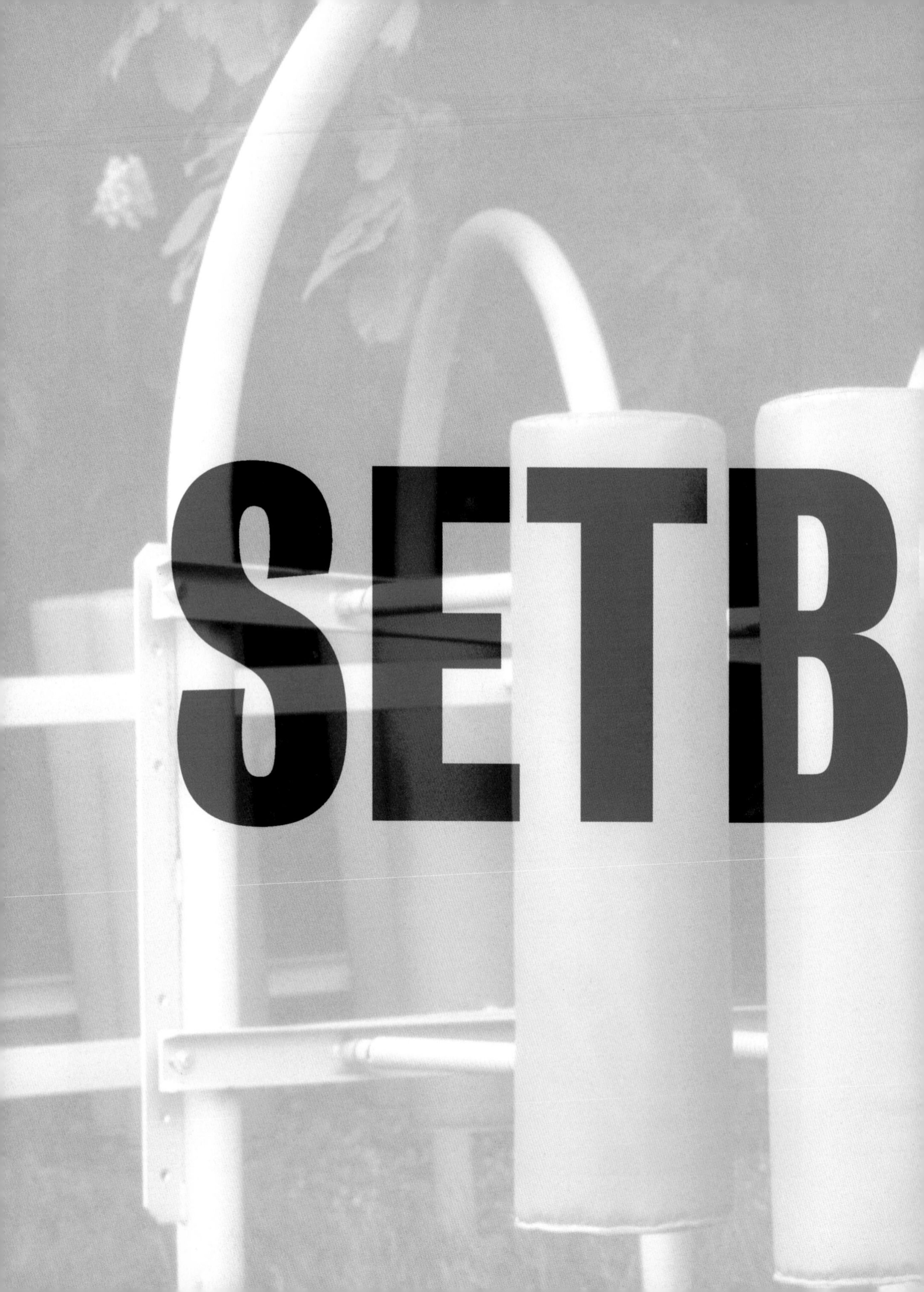

SETB

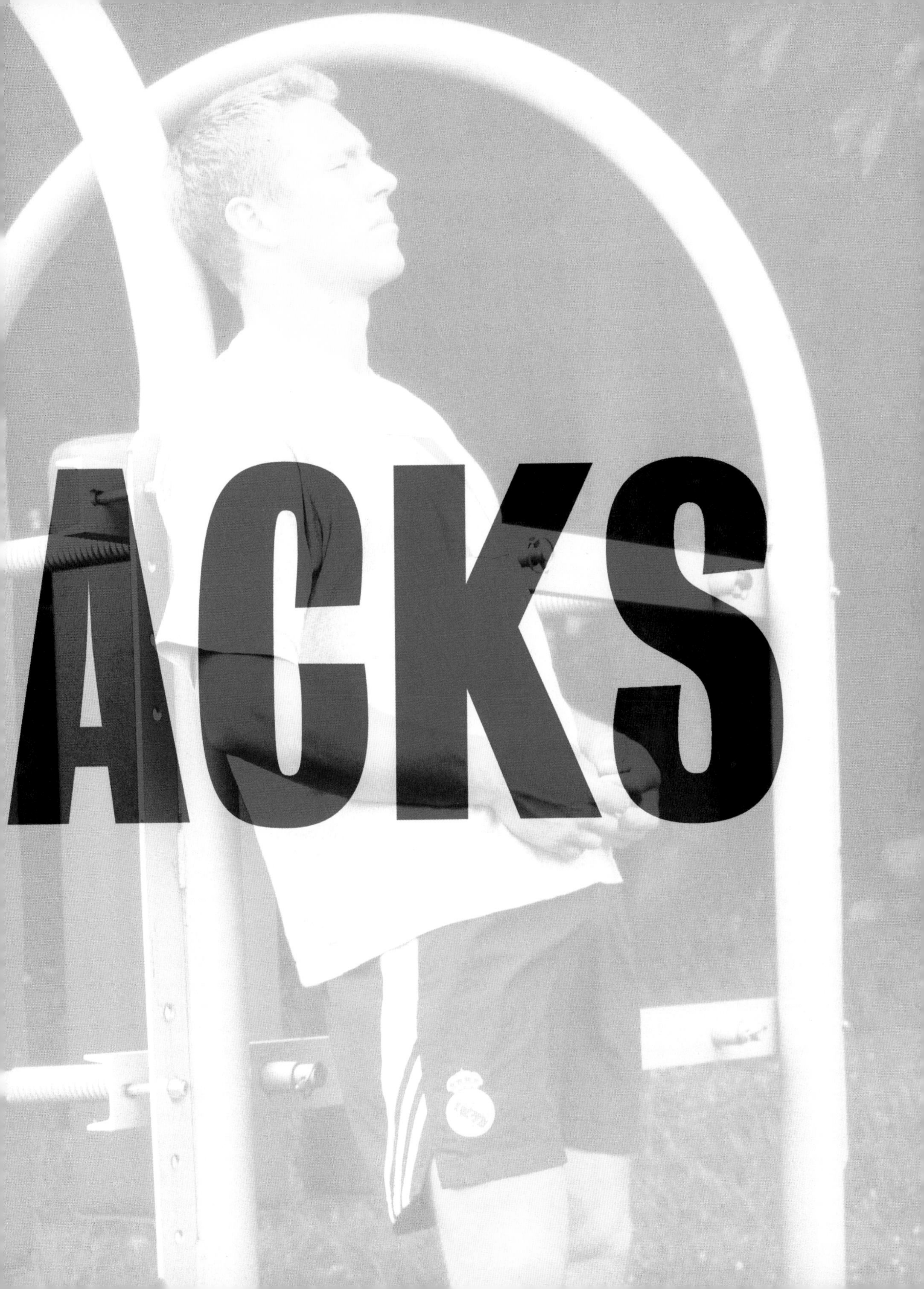
ACKS

"Challenges are what make life interesting; overcoming them is what makes life meaningful"

Joshua J. Marine

remember sitting in my hotel room in Brisbane after England had lost 76-0 to Australia in 1998 and crying my eyes out. I was on the phone to my dad, telling him what a nightmare the whole experience had been. My first game at fly-half for my country and a record Test defeat – what could have been worse?

I was only eighteen and it was still early in my career. In time I would realise that watching Australia go about their business brought home to me that I still had an awful lot further to go to become as good as those Wallabies. They were where I wanted to be and I resolved to use the experience of seeing the level players like Tim Horan were operating at to develop. But in the immediate aftermath of the thrashing I just felt desolate.

Dad waited for the sniffing to stop, then encouraged me not to let the disappointment beat me but to get up the next day and come back stronger. I had heard the advice before. It was exactly the same thing he said to me when, as a fourteen-year-old, I didn't get picked for Surrey's age-group side.

Different stage, but equally valid. If you get knocked down, make sure you get straight back up again.

That county setback felt like the end of the world at the time. When my dad passed on the bad news in the car park I was very upset. But after I had settled down, I resolved to show them what they were missing. Living on the county border, I also qualified to play for Hampshire so I went along to their trial a few weeks later and got into their side instead.

Hampshire wasn't the most fashionable of counties, and when it came to selection for the England Schools setup at under-sixteens level I was put on the bench and left there for the entire course of both games. So I rolled up my sleeves and fought my way into the under-eighteens 'A' side the following season, a year early. But when it came to England under-eighteens the next year I again missed out. In the end, an injury opened the door for me and I ended up playing alongside a big centre from Yorkshire called Mike Tindall and a whippet from Lancashire by the name of Iain Balshaw, but my experience of the trials system left a bitter taste.

The level playing field of professional rugby, where it didn't matter what school you had gone to or how well-connected you were, gave me what I wanted – the chance to prove they had got it badly wrong. Everyone has similar facilities and opportunities; it is up to each individual how hard he works to make the most of them. I resolved to work harder than anyone else and, with everyone at Newcastle's help, made my way into the full England side. In hindsight, I think having what I perceived to be a rough ride was good for me. A lot of players who achieve success early find it hard to maintain their inner drive at senior level. Because I wasn't handed the chances I thought I deserved, I fought all the more to earn them.

If you get knocked down, make sure you get straight back up again

Having made the England side, I wanted to make sure I kept the jersey. The worst part of the 76-0 drubbing was not the actual defeat but what happened afterwards. When the England squad for the autumn internationals that year

Perhaps I just wasn't ready for Test rugby then but I felt I had let myself and the people around me down

was announced, I wasn't in it. There wasn't so much as a phone call from Clive, so I was obviously a long way away from his thoughts. Perhaps I just wasn't ready for Test rugby then but I felt I had let myself and the people around me down. After all, I was in the England squad before the tour and clearly my performances in the southern hemisphere hadn't been good enough to make me indispensable. Grabbing every opportunity that presents itself is extremely important to me and this was a bad setback.

Faced with a punch in the guts you can either take the easy option in response or the hard one. My knee-jerk reaction was to hit club rugby at Newcastle with renewed venom and show Clive I was worthy of a place in his squad. It paid off. When the 1999 Five Nations' squad was announced two months later I was back in.

Since then I have only been dropped once by England – for the 1999 World Cup quarter-final. I was on the bench and I still had an important part to play in the second half when I came on for Paul Grayson, but Clive's decision meant he couldn't trust me when it mattered most. I understood his point, but I thought he was wrong. I had to persuade him to have more faith in my ability to control a game. I had to shed the 'inexperienced' tag which dogged me and the only way to do that was to play more matches. Fortunately, Newcastle was invaluable in terms of my learning. Playing outside Rob Andrew when I first arrived at the club gave me an insight into the ruthlessness with which he went about the job. He called the shots and the rest of us obeyed. With Rob's help and the wise guidance of Steve Bates I improved my level of influence on the field and, touch wood, while I have made mistakes, Clive hasn't felt the need to leave me out again since.

While a player can do something about form and therefore, to a degree, selection, there is nothing he can do about injury.

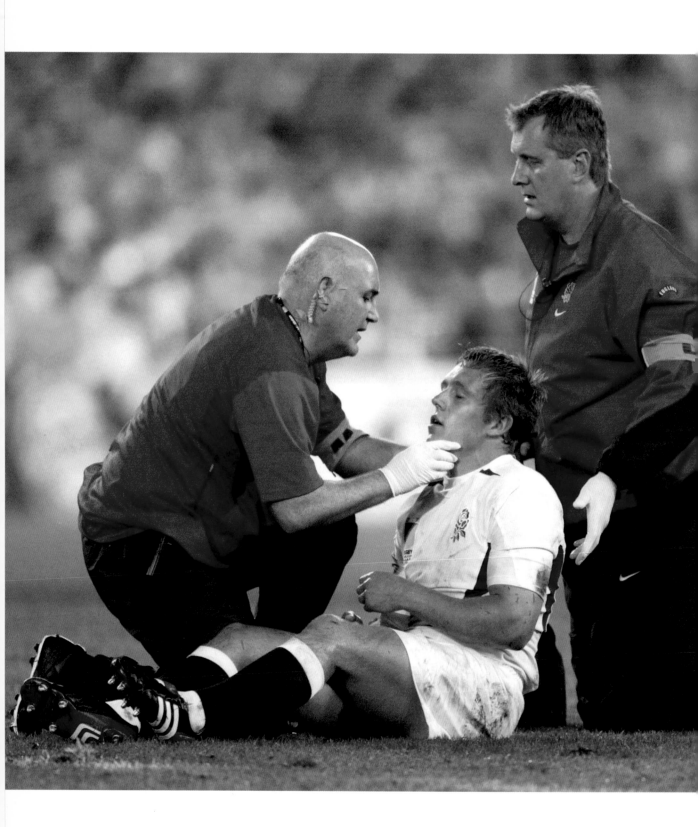

I knew there was a problem. The pain was much worse than before

When I tackled Matt Giteau in the first half of the final it went again, this time badly. I wasn't sure at first if I could continue. I stayed down for a long time because I couldn't move my arm. The paralysis brought temporary panic but as it eased off and feeling returned I was able to get up and get on with the game.

I took a few weeks off when we came home. An X-ray showed I had a fracture in a bone in my neck. It was an old injury which was healing and a red herring to the root cause of my stinger problem.

By the time I made my comeback for Newcastle, I thought the condition had settled down. However, when I tried to tackle John Clarke, the Northampton wing, fifty minutes into the game, I came off second best by a considerable margin. As I lay on the ground with play continuing downfield, I knew there was a problem. The pain was much worse than before. It was like a siren going off in my head. The familiar burning sensation down my right arm was hotter than I had ever known it, coming in great pulsating waves. I couldn't move my arm at all. Because I had taken a bang to the head in the tackle as well, I wasn't all there for a while. I was concussed and I couldn't think clearly. I was very concerned. After five minutes I was helped off and gingerly made my way round to the dressing rooms but it wasn't until well over an hour later that I regained feeling in my arm.

Even when I had recovered, I couldn't move it in certain directions and as the days went on matters worsened. Three of the smaller muscles in my arm just died on me. There was nothing there. The nerve that transmitted the message to them to tell them to grow had been damaged one too many times and now refused to work at all, shutting down completely. I sat and watched the muscles disappear in front of my eyes and there was nothing I could do about it.

Because it was to take place so close to the spinal cord, the surgery carried a tiny risk of permanent paralysis

I had two choices – to wait and hope the nerve would sort itself out or to have an operation to free it up to grow again. The problem was I couldn't wait forever for nature, not just because I would be missing more and more matches, but because the longer the delay the greater the chance of the nerve never recovering.

However, the operation carried elements of risk. The nerve might be irrevocably damaged by the procedure and because it was to take place so close to the spinal cord, the surgery carried a tiny risk of permanent paralysis. It was a one in a thousand chance but the surgeon was duty bound to tell me.

This scared me, but the decision was a no-brainer in the end. The improvement was coming far too slowly and I didn't know when it might stop for good. I had to go for the operation. Having made the decision I never really considered the paralysis outcome but I did worry that the operation would not work properly and that somehow I would have to modify my game to account for the fact that I would have no muscles on my right side. I thought about how I might change my tackling and passing techniques but I couldn't imagine hitting an opponent with any other motivation than to knock him into next week.

The operation left a neat, inch-long vertical scar down the back of my neck. As well as removing the bone spur, the surgeon widened the canal along which the nerve runs so there would be less chance of it jarring against anything in future.

It was a success – I was back training within a few days – but the nerve stubbornly refused to grow back as fast as I wanted it to. The weeks grew into months and the Six Nations' absence I had been told to resign myself to spread into a summer tour off as well.

I found out that being a squad member but not being involved in a big victory is very hard

Not playing does odd things to your head. It is funny how quickly you can begin to doubt yourself. When Newcastle contested the Powergen Cup final against Sale, it had only been five months since I had played against Australia at Telstra Stadium. Yet I had completely forgotten what it felt like to be involved in a final in front of thousands of people. I was as tense as if I had been playing, but whereas I would normally have channeled all that nervous energy into my own performance, I could find no outlet for it. As I watched from the side, ready to bring the water and messages on for the boys, I found myself marvelling at how well they were handling all the pressure and wondering whether I was capable of coping with it again. I was so relieved when we won a helter-skelter final I nearly exploded. When the boys set off on their lap of honour around Twickenham I watched them go with a great deal of pride but also with sadness. I wanted to have earned the right to go on it with them. I found out that being a squad member but not being involved in a big victory is very hard. It only adds to the enormous respect I have for the guys in the thirty at the World Cup who did not play in the final.

I hooked up with the Newcastle team for the celebrations in a London hotel afterwards but I made my excuses and left early. I was still feeling a little down and in any case I had to be up early to start the London Marathon in the morning. There were three more very clear clues that it was about time to go:

1. Mark Mayerhofler and Epi Taione were doing a Haka on the dance floor without any shirts on.
2. Steve Black was performing an 'erotic' dance on his own in the middle of the dance floor.
3. Stuart Grimes and our young flanker Ed Williams were literally ripping the shirts off each other's backs. It wouldn't have been so bad if it hadn't been taking place a matter of feet away from the sponsors who had kindly supplied the Hugo Boss shirts and suits to the squad for the final.

Playing for England can be stressful at times and tough to deal with but I know now it isn't half as painful as not playing for them

Watching England on the television was no better. Even though watching a couple of the Six Nations games with my dad took me back to my childhood, I was too close to it all to revert to being an armchair fan. I found myself living the match without the ability to alter the outcome. Horrible. Playing for England can be stressful at times and tough to deal with but I know now it isn't half as painful as not playing for them.

I missed everything about England. It is a fantastic environment to be involved in, both in terms of the professionalism and the people. Every aspect of our preparation is catered for, from the physical and nutritional side to the technical analysis of our opponents and ourselves. Every training session is videoed and a computer logs every step we take on the field.

The attention to detail is superb. For instance, at the World Cup, Clive used to send Richard Prescott, the RFU's communications director, along to the ground with the kickers when we practiced to ensure we weren't disturbed. For someone like me, who doesn't enjoy saying no to people, having someone on hand who does this for a living makes life so much easier. Richard's brief also included looking out for any suspicious camera-wielding opposition spies. And he still found time to fetch the balls for us.

With the RFU's backing, Clive has provided everything we could possibly want, from great hotels and facilities to specialist coaching in all important areas – some that we had never even considered. Sherylle Calder, a visual awareness expert from South Africa, works with us on improving our peripheral vision so we can pick out colleagues and space more effectively in the hurly-burly of a Test match. We spend at least twenty minutes per day when we are with England on computers, exercising our eyes. This is innovative and people are instinctively cautious when it comes to new ideas, but if you think about it, we use our eyes all the time in matches so something that makes them better makes us better. We are always looking for that edge.

Then there are the shirts. One of the more bizarre sights in the England dressing room is the rigmarole involved in helping people in and out of the new streamlined jerseys. They are so tight that it takes two or three people to do the job. The idea

is to stop opponents grabbing a trailing shirt. I can't wear the ultra-tight one – it is just too restrictive – so I wear the flared version, which is still almost like a second skin.

Even though it is an ultra-professional setup, the social environment is extremely relaxed and friendly. The England squad is a much more welcoming place now than it was when I made my debut. Playing international rugby is a serious business, but the tension which surrounds it needs a release and often laughter is the answer.

Dave 'Otis' Reddin, England fitness conditioner and a former non-league footballer, is my keepie-uppie partner. Early on in a Test week, or the day after a game, we take over one of the dining rooms in the swanky Pennyhill Park Hotel and re-assign it for indoor football trick shots, each of which is given a code name. It is quite warm in there. Quite what the waiters think when they poke their heads around the door and find two sweaty men lying on the floor trying to flick the ball into the air with their backsides – the hitherto unachievable Northern Soul – I don't know.

Anyway, at the World Cup, Otis was at the centre of a disciplinary storm when England were discovered to have briefly but mistakenly put sixteen men on the field against Samoa. It was a serious matter. Clive had been summoned to fly to Sydney from Surfers Paradise to answer the charges and there were even calls for points deductions. Otis was the man who had given the instruction from the touchline for Dan Luger to go on and consequently become the notorious sixteenth man and this had led to an altercation with the fourth official, Steve Walsh from New Zealand, in which Walsh reportedly called Otis a '****ing loser'. When we met to draw up our defence, every time Otis's name was mentioned so was the insult. Without fail, on hearing it, we all collapsed like kids in a playground.

Before our World Cup warm-up match in Marseilles in 2003 we had some light relief at our French training camp with some backs against forwards football. The backs cruised to victory, of course, due to the appalling work rate of the forwards – idleness that was only matched on our side by Will Greenwood. To compound our justified sense of superiority we also cantered clear in the penalty shoot-out which followed. Two penalties each and the forwards did not score a single goal. However,

> # Playing international rugby is a serious business, but the tension which surrounds it needs a release and often laughter is the answer

that didn't matter to Phil Vickery who pulled off a remarkable, and I have to stress totally inadvertent, save from my second penalty. Having gone for the top right-hand corner with the first one but curled it just over the bar of the five-a-side goal we were using, I decided to go for pure power with the second. I really connected. The ball smashed into the post just below the bar and, with Vicks cowering away, ricocheted across square onto the top of the shaven noggin. He's a big bloke but he went down like a sack of spuds. For a moment I thought the ball had knocked him out but he looked up with a big smile because the ball had stayed out of the net.

This was vaguely reminiscent of an incident that occurred two days before we played South Africa in 2000. We were attempting to perfect the cross-field kick to the corner for Ben Cohen and Richard Hill, a move that was to pay rich dividends for England. The line-out had been set fifteen yards further back than the move was suitable for so, to put the ball into the in-goal area with time for them to arrive and catch it, I had to give the ball everything and put plenty of height on it. Unfortunately, the sun was directly behind me as I hit what is still the sweetest punt of my life. Hilly arrived and was temporarily blinded. The ball came down with snow on it right on top of his head and cannoned back into the air. It was then that Ben leapt beautifully to take the ball above his head and touch down, much to the delight of Dave Alred, who doubles as our catching coach. Five points, one man down and an outbreak of mass hysteria – even Clive was bent double.

The bizarre backdrop to the successful World Cup campaign was a spate of trouser attacks by our reserve hooker Mark Regan

You can't beat slapstick. The bizarre backdrop to the successful World Cup campaign was a spate of trouser attacks by our reserve hooker Mark Regan. 'Ronnie' started an unfortunate trend by whipping down the shorts of Josh Lewsey at Perth Airport as he was trying on a pair of sunglasses. Unfortunately, Josh hadn't got any pants on.

As we moved on to Brisbane other people started to get in on the act. A training session in a school gymnasium ended in disaster for Dan Luger when he put his arms in the air to line up the perfect swan dive into a deep foam-filled pit, giving Cohen an opportunity to take advantage of his vulnerability and take down his shorts. Dan sported the same underwear as Josh – i.e. none – and as he scrabbled about to restore his dignity, Ben shoved him over onto the crash mat with his shorts still round his ankles. Unfortunately, the gym was also being used by some schoolchildren and a couple of irate mothers, watching the hi-jinx from the balcony, gave Ben a severe ticking off. Incredibly, Dan copped one too.

Ronnie was untouchable as the master of the clandestine assault, though, and as the tournament progressed he peaked magnificently. He pulled off a spectacular attack on the team doctor, Simon Kemp, in full view of all the photographers, during a training session before the semi-final. He finished the assault by inappropriately slapping the doctor's exposed backside. Alert to the danger and aware that the odd lens might be on me, I pulled my drawstring so tight it was in danger of cutting off the circulation to my legs. As if there wasn't enough tension around.

Ronnie's piéce de resistance came after the final when we were doing our lap of honour around Telstra Stadium. You would have thought the distraction of winning the World Cup would have kept anyone's mind off the potential for trouser comedy but that reckoned without the dedication of the man. Down came the shorts of Simon Shaw in front of a global audience of countless millions.

Playing rugby for my country is what being with England is ultimately about but to me guys like these are England. Turning up at our team hotel on an international week and seeing close friends like Hilly and Catty sets off the unique tingle of Test rugby – all the hype, all the planning, all the tension is embodied in those people. Even running into them as opponents at club level brings the same instinctive surge of electricity. When we've retired and we meet up we'll probably still feel it.

Looking in at England from the outside was made worse by their defeats in the Six Nations and on the summer tour.

England cannot win every match, however much they'd like to, and the losses to Ireland and France left us third in the final Six Nations table. It was a desperately difficult tournament so soon after the World Cup. I know what I went through and I wasn't even playing. As some familiar faces stepped aside, I can only imagine how difficult it was mentally for those who remained to switch from the adulation that followed the World Cup win to the task of facing our European rivals with points to prove. Facing huge ovations before matches rather than after them is an awkward position to find yourself in.

Down came the shorts of Simon Shaw in front of a global audience of countless millions

As with individuals, it is not the victories but the setbacks which truly shape a team

Australia and New Zealand was hardly a picnic either, especially when you consider our guys had been at it solidly for twelve months, while the southern hemisphere's season had ended after the World Cup.

More than the physical exhaustion, I think England were victims of the expectations which surrounded them as world champions. The experiences Down Under will have underlined how hard it is to live up to them if you take your eye off the ball even for a second.

Australia and New Zealand are difficult places for European sides to go in June at the best of times, and the three defeats only served to emphasis what an achievement it had been winning in both two years before.

I watched the matches at home and spoke to guys like Hilly, Mike Catt and Ben Cohen to find out how they were doing and how they were feeling. It seemed a tough tour. I think England were very unlucky with Simon Shaw's sending off in the second Test against the All Blacks, which had a big influence on the outcome, but in the first Test against New Zealand and against the Wallabies it was hard going and we were beaten very fairly.

Our defensive standards slipped – letting in fourteen tries in three Tests is very unlike England – and we didn't create as much as we would have liked to in attack. If it proved anything, the tour probably showed that we have to be prepared to speculate to accumulate and take risks. Both New Zealand and Australia had attacking threats in every back-line position and players in the forwards who could do real damage with the ball too.

In the long term I believe these experiences will definitely not do England any harm. As with individuals, it is not the victories but the setbacks which truly shape a team and provide the biggest avenues for improvement. Those harrowing Grand Slam defeats at Wembley, Murrayfield and Lansdowne Road in 1999, 2000 and 2001 were the making of England. We learned from those experiences and that is what made us the side we were when it came to facing Australia in Sydney in 2003. This new England side is starting down the same road and I, along with everyone else, am looking forward to hopefully being part of the next journey.

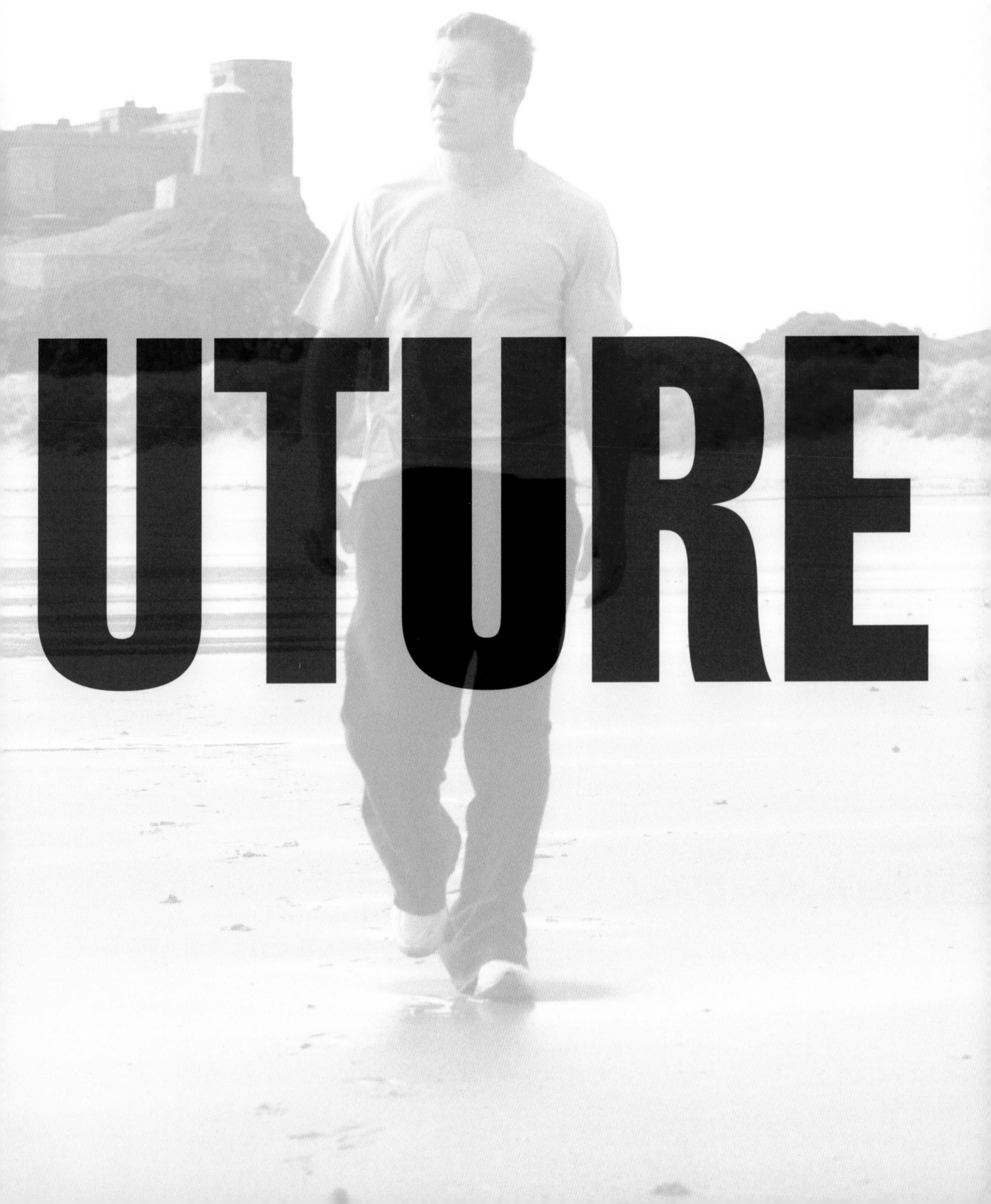
UTURE

'A person who aims at nothing is sure to hit it'

Anon

Winning the World Cup fulfilled a promise I made to myself when I was ten. Most children write out Christmas lists for Santa – I wrote out a list of goals I wanted to achieve as a rugby player.

I began to think about what would come next about an hour after the World Cup final. While the celebrations continued in the changing room, I found peace in the physio area. With ice on my neck and elbow, I went through in my head what had enabled me to be part of a team that had just won a World Cup. I thought about everything that had gone into that game, what we had achieved and where I wanted to go next. More importantly, I began to work out how I was going to get there.

It would have been so easy to bask in the reflected glory of what the team had done and take my eye off the ball – maybe to train a little less intensely or skip a few kicks at the end of a session. I didn't want to view 22 November 2003 as an end point. I'm guessing it will form the background noise to the rest of my career, my life maybe, but I want it to be a stepping stone to further achievements.

The injury and the operation provided an unwanted detour from the path I had begun to set down, but at the same time they supplied a clear dividing line between the past and the future. During the flight to Mauritius to start my recuperation, I wrote down a new list of goals in a black notebook. It is a more detailed, clearer look at my future than ever before, covering my club and international rugby and also my life. Here are a few examples.

SHORT-TERM GOALS:

To come back physically stronger, more powerful and in better shape
than ever before, making myself the fittest player in world rugby.

To improve my defensive technique and communication.

To improve all my skills by a large amount, specifically my
passing and kicking.

To improve my quality of training to ensure I get the best
out of my effort.

To make sure my diet and nutrition is as effective and professional as it
can possibly be.

To enjoy playing the game of rugby a great deal more.

My operation gave me a lot of time off and I could have switched off from rugby completely. Mentally, I suppose a break would have been refreshing. However, I know that if I had taken the time off, I would have looked back and regretted it. In rugby's crowded calendar, there are so few opportunities to work on your conditioning that the time away from playing matches was actually a godsend. In the past, I had merely maintained my levels of strength and fitness because there was no time to do anything else. The off-season, such as it was, meant a couple of weeks' holiday and then straight back to pre-season work. The enforced break from playing I was now faced with meant I was able to drive myself up to a new level. To maintain some balance, I made sure I trained hard but relaxed even harder in the evenings.

Following the operation and the subsequent training I went through to get back to full fitness, I may have to modify my technique a little in some of my skills to take account of the inevitable physical changes, but this is just another challenge for me to embrace.

Overall, physically I am way ahead of where I was. I now weigh fourteen stone and my body fat levels are down to nine per cent. I can lift heavier weights, I can recover more quickly after pushing myself to the limit – every aspect of my conditioning has improved.

This is going to help with my tackling. It is an important part of my game and I want to make myself more effective in this area. I have set myself a target of five big hits per game. I won't always reach it – the overriding aim for me is to finish each match with a 100 per cent tackle success rate – but the heavy collisions are the ones that can really lift a team.

My right side will probably always be slightly weaker than my left

I think I can kick better too. I was really disappointed with my punting, particularly from my left foot, at the World Cup – my right was probably thirty per cent better – so I have set out to try to rectify the disparity. During my time off, I put myself through more sessions than I would have done if I had been playing. When Newcastle took the posts down at Kingston Park at the end of the season for an event on the field, I asked them to leave one up so I could carry on. Like a mechanic in a garage, I stripped down my goal-kicking technique and gradually built it back up again. I enjoy the process of self-analysis. If I kick nine goals out of ten, I will devote all my time to working out why I missed one, rather than why I was successful with nine. Some people might find this approach negative but the aim is to try to eliminate as many mistakes as possible for next time. For me, playing sport at a high level is largely about handling the mental side and

the only way I can do this is to have a routine I can trust. Only robots aren't affected by tension. I've faced kicks when the anxiety has been so great I could actually see my heart beating through my shirt. I've been at the end of my run-up and felt like my legs had dissolved under me. But if I've put the hours in I know the chances are that I will be able to confront and control the demons.

I do a lot of practice – it is what my whole game is based upon – but having done so I have come to realise that I should try to get something more out of rugby than just winning. While I don't intend to drop my concentration and intensity levels, I want to embrace the experience more. I no longer want to feel relieved to come off the field; I want to enjoy actually being out on the pitch. If I can smile when I'm out there, express myself better and come out of myself then I believe I can unlock more of what I have to give.

I have a set of long-term goals. I wrote those down too. Here they are:

To win the World Cup again with England and be a major influence in the side that does it.

To be selected for the British and Irish Lions tour to New Zealand in 2005 and to have an influence on a successful trip.

To play as many games as possible for England, injury allowing.

To win more Grand Slams.

To be the best prepared rugby player in the world.

To play at my very best in every match – not just the big ones – so as to be a leader in consistency as well as performance.

To train at my very best in every session. Never to accept that bad days just happen. To make every day a good day.

To help my brother develop into the player he wants to be and play with him regularly in the Newcastle team.

Personal milestones, like points tallys and numbers of caps, aren't really important. People make a fuss about them, but if records come along they are essentially spin-offs of training and playing to your best. One leads to the other. They would be

> **If I can smile when I'm out there then I believe I can unlock more of what I have to give**

I've faced kicks when the anxiety has been so great I could actually see my heart beating through my shirt

good to look back on when I have retired, but that's about it. When Jason Leonard broke the world record for international caps against France in the World Cup semi-final we presented him with a ball and a shirt numbered 112 after his record number of caps. It was an incredible feat, after all, for a guy who had had part of his pelvis grafted onto his neck to save his career a decade before. Jase was quite embarrassed about all the hullabaloo. What mattered to him was that we had reached the final. I want to look at records the same way. The individual achievements are only important in so much as they mean I have contributed to the side's success. A man of the match award in a losing team is utterly worthless. Even in a winning side, they do not mean much. The point of the exercise is not the physical prize but the inner satisfaction of knowing the goal has been achieved. I have a few awards at home – unopened champagne bottles, that sort of thing – and I feel very honoured. I have no idea where my World Cup winners' medal is, though. My dad put it somewhere for safekeeping, I think. I must ask him.

The long-term goal that would mean the most to me is the one involving my brother. He has always been there for me and I want to be there for him as he continues to carve his own professional career at Newcastle.

We are unusually close. His abstract take on life and bizarre sense of humour make me laugh. We chuckle at a lot of the same things, whether that is the weirdly amusing *Garth Marenghi's Dark Place*, the wise-cracking *Simpsons*, the slapstick of an old *Young Ones* episode or a *Fantasy Football* Phoenix From the Flames skit. I know people probably regard me as quite earnest and older than my years – and I do take my job and everything that surrounds it very seriously – but when I'm at home with Sparks it is a pathetically juvenile environment. There's a non-stop stream of banter flowing between us which we find incredibly funny. That's just as well because no-one else does.

To win a
trophy in the
same side as
Sparks would
be as special a
moment as I
can imagine on
a rugby field

Unlike most brothers, we don't really argue. Perhaps that is because, although we train together, we never play games against each other – not even computer games. When we were growing up we might have knocked up on a tennis court for three hours at a time, working on serve and volley or passing shots, but there was never a match. Perhaps we feared the consequences. We are both fiercely competitive. The last time we took each other on was on the computer when I was ten. Sparks is seventeen months older and used his extra experience to give me a sound beating which I reacted to by storming off to the rhubarb patch at the bottom of our garden and sulking there for forty-five minutes.

I've forgiven him now. To win a trophy in the same side as Sparks would be as special a moment as I can imagine on a rugby field.

For that to happen, Newcastle have to develop as a side and as a club. My goals for the Falcons, which I also wrote down in the black book, are as follows:

To win the Zurich Premiership.

To win it again.

To win the Powergen Cup.

To win the Heineken Cup.

To dominate the game in England and Europe for several years.

To lead the club in our quest.

If you shoot for the moon, even if you miss you'll land amongst the stars.

Perhaps because of where we are geographically, on the far reaches of the professional circuit in England, Newcastle is a very close-knit and friendly club. We have a great time together. At the end of last season, all the players who were staying on clubbed together to buy mementoes for all those who were leaving. They received them at our end-of-season get-together at Kingston Park. Garath Archer, who was forced to retire because of a back injury, went up to collect his award and gave an incredibly moving acceptance speech. Naked.

In performance terms the most important area we have to improve on is our defence

I want more than just laughs from my club career, though; I want Newcastle to become winners. We have a decent team, a stadium at Kingston Park built from scratch and a great crowd filling it. What we haven't yet created is a winning mentality and a winning habit. We came out the wrong side in numerous close games last season.

In performance terms the most important area we have to improve on is our defence. Last season we were a top four side in the number of tries we scored but near the relegation zone in the number we conceded. I want our defence to equal that of a world-class international team by raising the levels of under-standing, enthusiasm and technique.

But that is only part of the challenge. What won England the World Cup was not how well we played – we performed better in a physical rugby sense nine months earlier in beating Australia and New Zealand away – but our mental strength. The whole team had supreme confidence that we would win those one- or two-point games. Our killer instinct was unparalleled – we had pretty much forgotten how to lose.

People ask why it is that other English sports teams or sportsmen have not won important titles. Not being involved directly it is difficult to say. From the outside it looked as though England's football team had prepared well enough to have gone on and won Euro 2004, only for them to lose the penalty shoot-out against Portugal. But while penalties are a lottery, I would just point out how important the confidence that comes from having won big games like that previously can be. If you know you can do it and trust your team-mates implicitly, there is almost a feeling of inevitability that you will come through. You cannot buy that reservoir of reassurance, that knowledge that even if the opposition opens up a lead you have the know-how to claw it back. The England football team had a good record prior to the tournament. While they were not quite able to build up enough of a winning habit for Euro 2004, if they continue the way they are going there is no reason why they cannot win the World Cup in two years' time.

Part of the reason we were able to do so was down to the personalities involved and the quality of the players, but also the environment we existed in. It was a no-excuse environment. We have a set of teamship rules with England, drawn up by the players, which govern our conduct and help to set standards in areas such as punctuality. On time for a meeting means ten minutes early, for instance.

I want to mirror that with Newcastle. The resources might not match those of the RFU but there is no reason why the approach cannot be the same. The winning habit has to be created from within and that impacts on all areas of preparation. Everyone at the club has a responsibility to be accountable for everything they do and how it affects the team.

I recognise not everyone is like me – it would be a particularly boring world if they were – but we all share the same desire for success. It's how far we are prepared to go to achieve it that will decide whether we get there.

I have been through a lot with Newcastle, both good and bad times. We have enjoyed great one-off success – the title delivered by the team of superstars Sir John Hall bought in and two cups in the space of four seasons. We have also endured some challenging lows – when we nearly folded before Dave Thompson stepped in as chairman and a horrible flirtation with relegation in 2002/3.

Loyalty is a big part of my make-up and I have been at Newcastle since I left school. I want to be part of building something. To me the end goal is only rewarding after strife and struggle. As long as I still think it is possible for the Falcons to reach the heights I am aiming for, I will give everything I have to the club to help us scale them. I passionately believe we can.

We have a set of teamship rules with England, drawn up by the players, which govern our conduct and help to set standards

I've chosen a narrow passage through life, trading my youth to challenge myself to become the best rugby player I can be

I have to chase goals. I have a lot of energy which needs channelling in a positive direction and ambitions are a key part of keeping me sane. I had a summer off a couple of years ago and without specific aims I found myself becoming bored. I was doing too much thinking and became too insular. I ate away at myself and became very gloomy. It was a paradox, but without something to strive for I couldn't relax. I began to wonder whether rugby had stopped fulfilling me and whether my all-consuming approach to it was the problem, when in reality it was the absence of rugby which was killing me. Once the new season arrived, I was fine.

Out of rugby for eight months following the operation, I could easily have gone the same way. Mapping out a set of goals I wanted to achieve and training towards them stopped that.

I widened the goal-setting approach beyond rugby. These are the personal aspirations I wrote down in my black book:

To become a better, more mature and developed person.
To work with charities and make a difference to the causes that are
    closest to me.
To learn the guitar and piano.
To become fluent in French and Spanish.
To stay true to the ideal of being able to sign off the video of my life.

I've chosen a narrow passage through life, trading my youth to challenge myself to become the best rugby player I can be. I haven't missed the hangovers – they're not really me – but there are things I regret not doing.

I found myself standing outside Newcastle University last summer, thinking how different my life would have been if I had taken up the place at Durham I was offered. When I was eighteen, I didn't feel I could combine my studies with rugby, and with my myopic approach I was probably right, but I know I passed up a

Forming a circle of friends away from rugby is something I haven't been able to do

life-enhancing opportunity. University would have been a wonderful experience, socially as much as anything. Forming a circle of friends away from rugby is something I haven't been able to do. I have so many great mates in rugby, but I suppose they can sometimes be like office colleagues. I know I can't recapture that time now – if I went back to uni to study when I was thirty-two it wouldn't be the same.

I'd also have loved to have taken a gap year and travelled as well. Playing rugby for England you fly around the world and stay in top hotels but all you tend to see are the insides of meeting rooms and training pitch after training pitch. I know it won't happen for a while but I'm looking forward to the day I can go exploring New Zealand and be treated exactly the same as every other English backpacker. That's a country I would like to see more of.

I had a rare chance to see some of the world in July 2004 on an adidas promotional tour to the Far East. The trip was an eye-opener in many ways. It was the first time I'd experienced an earthquake for a start. There I was, minding my own business, in my hotel in Tokyo, signing a few bits and pieces, when everything in the room started rattling.

'What's that?' I asked Duncan, the cameraman who was with me, alarmed.

'That would be a tremor,' he replied. It turned out he had been on the receiving end of one before in Mexico.

'How did that turn out?' I asked.

'Pretty badly,' he said.

The room, which was on the ninth floor, began to sway and shake. The walls seemed to be bending in front of my eyes.

'Should we head downstairs?' I asked.

'That would be probably be best,' he said.

Even though I was in a potentially bad situation, where time was clearly of the essence, I found myself searching for my trainers and the lid to my pen before we evacuated. Sometimes I despair of myself.

By the time the door had shut behind us, the strange, shifting sensation had died away. In the corridor I had with me the pen lid and my trainers but not my room key. We had to head down to reception for another one to get back in.

One of the locals estimated the tremor to have measured three on the Richter Scale, nothing special by Tokyo standards but quite enough for me.

The cultural differences are what immediately strike you when you travel but sometimes it is what we have in common which can cause the problems. I was due to have dinner with senior adidas management in Japan. I needed to visit the gents beforehand but was confused by what I came across when I got there. The toilet had a button on the side, which I presumed must be for flushing. I pressed it and in a classic piece of slapstick it squirted water at me. Drawn like a rabbit to a car's headlights, I had another two or three stabs at the same button and soaked myself in the process. Only then, as I prepared to meet my sponsors dripping wet, did I see the correct button on the top of the toilet. Exactly where you would find it at home, of course.

Singapore was wet too, for a different reason. The humidity. Walking along the street was like taking a shower. I tried washing away the sweat but it was almost counter-productive. I sweated even more after taking a shower. In the end I simply gave up and turned up at the airport for my flight after a moist game of basketball looking like I had been swimming. Not great for my fellow passengers. The basketball – a head-to-head dunking competition with an adidas guy called Dave – had ended in high drama when he pulled off the hoop and the glass backboard by mistake mid-shot and it ended up crashing down around him.

Rather than ruining local basketball facilities, the idea of the tour was to carry out kicking clinics for youngsters. Hong Kong was memorable. Fifty children from local clubs had been rounded up to take part, and in front of them and around 500 spectators I went through a training drill with them. I was wired up to a microphone throughout so the kids could hear what I was saying. Despite some wind, the punting went off OK, but there was a marked lack of response from them as I told them what I was trying to do. They just looked blank. I thought I was maybe being too technical so I toned it down as I went into my goal-kicking routine. Still nothing. 'Tough audience,' I thought. By the time it came to my last kick, a shot at goal at a very narrow angle, I knew I needed a top one to win them over. I hit it perfectly and through the eye of the needle it went. Triumphantly, I looked across – at the same sea of impassive faces. Only later did I find out that they didn't speak English.

A translator was provided to help out in Japan. I did the same routine for a group of very talented players from the Waseda University team in Tokyo. I had generally kicked well out there but for some reason the radar had gone haywire for ten minutes in my own two-hour session that morning. It put me on edge a little as the kicking clinic, the real reason for me being there, approached. The presentation went well and when it came to the big finale the first kick I lined up from a tight

One of the locals estimated the tremor to have measured three on the Richter scale, nothing special by Tokyo standards but quite enough for me

The Japanese love their rugby and are exciting and skilful players too

angle five metres from the goal line scraped the post. The next three all went through the middle.

However as I lined up my penultimate kick the wind speed increased. 'When the wind picks up,' I told the students through the translator, 'it's important to aim for a spot to one side and to stick to it rather than trying to bend the ball in. The wind will do that for you.' Message conveyed, I promptly struck a ball which never deviated an inch straight into the far post. 'However sometimes the wind drops,' I added. After a nervous wait for the translation, it transpired my line had gone down OK.

I coached some five- to eight-year-olds in Tokyo as well. They were fantastic - all decked out in their white or red scrum caps. They did this drill where they all lined up around a basket and kicked balls into it. I found out where the scrum caps came in when they overshot and peppered each others' heads with stray balls. None of them batted an eyelid.

From what I experienced of Japan, it would be a good place to host a future rugby World Cup. The Japanese love their rugby and are exciting and skilful players too. As a country to visit it would be great for the fans as well - a vivid and memorable experience. I loved the place. One of my most prized possessions is now a Waseda University shirt signed in Japanese symbols by the team.

I studied languages at school and I have started to revisit my French text books of late. France is another place that interests me — it's so close and yet the approach to life seems so different. I'm quite envious of guys like Dan Luger who have gone across the Channel to play and who are picking up the language and getting to understand the country and its people.

Africa is another part of the globe I'd like to spend some time in. I have this dream of going off to work in a game park when I finish playing. I'm used to the outdoor life but I imagine it would be so different to the regimented lifestyle I have chosen for myself, being woken by the chatter of the monkeys and the distant roar of a lion. There's something thrilling and basic about the idea of living amongst animals in their own environment. The nearest I get at the moment is visiting Mike Tindall's room with England. A cheap shot, I know, but I owe him for claiming on television that he was standing in for me at an awards show because they couldn't afford my appearance fee.

Post-rugby, I know I'll have to find something to do which satisfies my need to achieve. I couldn't imagine doing a job which did not make a difference. Coaching may be one avenue worth exploring. My brief taste as Newcastle defence coach while I was injured was an experience I found interesting, if worrying. You can't really practice defence properly without physical contact and I was scared stiff in case anyone was hurt and missed a match. I must admit I did really enjoy seeing the penny drop on the occasions I managed to get my message across. I know from the other side of the fence how helpful it is when you are struggling with something and a coach comes up with the answer. I also did some kicking coaching last season with a couple of very good students – Paul Gascoigne and Peter Beardsley. They were playing as celebrity goal-kickers in a charity match at Kingston Park and were unjustly worried that they might make fools of themselves,

When my body tells me it is time to give up and I am no longer moving forward as a player, I will go

so we did a little work together at Darsley Park. We aimed at a post from twenty metres away for one training drill and Gazza hit it three times in a row. When it came to the match, Gazza landed five out of six while Peter managed nine out of ten including the last one with his left foot. What a teacher! In fact they were just naturals.

Or maybe I could do something charity-related. I was honoured to be made an ambassador of the NSPCC. Family is hugely important to me — one day I would like to have a big family of my own — so trying to help children who are less fortunate is something I care deeply about. Kylie is also an ambassador. I haven't met her yet but I do need a word. There is a vocalist spot going in the Wilkinson band which she might want to audition for.

I first picked up a guitar with my Newcastle colleague Jamie Noon a couple of years ago to try to find a way to switch off from rugby. As I have progressed I have become more and more engrossed in it. I can play to a reasonable level now and, with my brother taking up the drums, we are able to have the odd jamming session in our noise room upstairs at home. I've also just inherited a piano from a friend and I'm determined to learn to play that properly too. Or a bit better than the England squad's resident pianist Joe Worsley anyway.

How long will I play rugby for? I remember talking to Inga Tuigamala about this. In his last season at Newcastle he was still a thundering force, but it was becoming harder for him and he felt the moment was right to step aside. He asked the coaching staff to drop him so the younger players who would eventually replace him could be given experience. They refused — he was too valuable to the side — but he could not accept seeing his standards fall, even if he was still an integral member of the team, and he gave it up to return home to New Zealand and concentrate on his young family at the end of the season.

When my body tells me it is time to give up and I am no longer moving forward as a player, I will go too. Martin Johnson showed how it should be done. Every professional sportsman would be envious of his farewell from Test rugby. It was a fairytale ending for him, to walk away from England after an unbeaten season, a Grand Slam and with the Webb Ellis Trophy under his arm.

At twenty-five, I know I'm only part of the way to becoming the player I want to be

There is no timescale on the rest of my career, only that I want to leave at the top, to step aside before my performances begin to deteriorate. That could be after the next World Cup when I will be twenty-eight or the one after when I will be thirty-two. The enforced lay-off may have added extra time on to the end of my career – who knows?

I can't say I will achieve all the goals I've set in whatever time is available, but what I can guarantee is I will give myself every chance. I have no excuse not to do the best I can because, as I've said before, I have it easy. Life has been put on a plate for me.

Off the field everything is taken care of. My parents have turned their own lives upside down by upping sticks and moving from Surrey to Northumberland to be on hand for me. Dad has given up his own career as a financial adviser to work full time managing and taking care of me to ensure that nothing ever interferes with my rugby. Alongside him, Tim Buttimore and Simon Cohen work to look after the commercial and legal side. A more trustworthy trio of people you could not wish to meet.

Blackie and Otis make sure I'm in top condition, Dave Alred is always there for me and my kicking, and all the coaches at Newcastle and England are continually helping me to move on as a player. All I have to do is turn up to train and play. If I didn't pay them back by giving my all, I don't know how I would live with myself.

I have recommitted to leaving no stone unturned in my quest to improve. I am having a gym installed at home. The design leaves a space for a patch of artificial grass on which to practise drop kicks. You never know when one might come in handy again.

The work goes on. Even though the World Cup has gone, I have too much unfinished business in rugby. At twenty-five, I know I'm only part of the way to becoming the player I want to be. As far as I am concerned, the slate is clean. Chapter one is over; chapter two of my career starts now.

Picture Credits

All photographs are © 2004 Harry Borden except as follows:

Getty Images: 14-15, 18, 20-21, 25, 26, 28-9, 30, 56, 59, 76-7, 81, 85, 134, 149, 152 (right), 153, 162, 193

Dave Rogers/Getty Images: 38, 87, 90 (right), 92, 96, 105, 110, 111, 114, 115, 118-19, 128, 129, 169, 172-3, 184-5, 188, 189

PA Photos: 40-41, 72, 73, 74-5, 79, 82, 90 (left), 91, 95, 175

Corbis: 43, 64-5, 67, 68-9, 140, 143, 144, 152 (left), 157

Tom Jenkins: 61, 70-71, 89, 166, 180-81

Empics: 62, 63, 66

Photography Paul Smith: 136-7

Fotopress: 170, 200, 203, 204, 207, 209

John Angerson, *The Times Magazine*: 190

Rex Features: 112

Jed Wee: 124, 194

Photographs courtesy of the Wilkinson family: 46, 47, 51, 154-5, 187